Waldorf Education:
An Introduction for Parents

Waldorf Education:
An Introduction for Parents

Printed with support from the Waldorf Curriculum Fund

Published by:
Waldorf Publications at the
Research Institute for Waldorf Education
38 Main Street
Chatham, NY 12037

Title: ***Waldorf Education: An Introduction for Parents***
Editor: David Mitchell
Layout: Ann Erwin

The material in this book was originally published as a series of four enrollment information brochures: The Waldorf Kindergarten, Waldorf: The Elementary Years, Waldorf and Adolescence, and the Results of Waldorf Education, all available from Waldorf Publications in their original format. www.waldorfpublications.org

Table of Contents

Foreword

Enrollment in a Waldorf School

Our work in Waldorf Publications is to find as many ways possible to be helpful in explaining this revolutionary approach to education so that any who are interested can get a real sense of the program.

With its unique view of child development, Waldorf education has not changed in over 90 years of success that it has enjoyed in North America. The basic understanding of the three seven-year periods that constitute a growing young person's educational years remains reliable. Within each seven-year period, though, the freedom granted to teachers to observe, design, and carry out an educational program creates many variations on predictable themes. These variations are designed by teachers to meet the needs of their particular groups of children, their classes. And so, change and variety are hallmarks of Waldorf education, even as the foundational view of child development remains stable and proves itself with every child.

Waldorf education increasingly deviates from mainstream imaginations of education. This is not because Waldorf education keeps changing, but because mainstream education has continued a rigorous adoption of electronic equipment, testing, and performance-oriented education with increasing pressure to perform reaching into lower and lower grades and even into kindergarten.

Though today's children still follow the same developmental paths, certainly the circumstances that surround them have changed dramatically in the last 90 years. In light of this, Waldorf education offers a stable and secure environment in which to learn and to discover the childlike answer to the age-old question, "Who am I?"

This book is a compilation of enrollment materials provided to Waldorf schools across North America to give interested families a good idea of what Waldorf education is, its mission, and how it accomplishes education for students at the different ages from kindergarten through high school.

The approach is through essays written by experienced teachers. Rich with ideas from the classroom, they can give parents more of a living characterization of Waldorf practices from real life situations and less theory. Our hope is that this collection will help the reader to understand Waldorf education more fully.

The four leaflets are also sold separately so that applicants for the early childhood program can read about that particular area and curriculum; likewise for elementary education and education for adolescents in a Waldorf school. For ordering additional copies of this book or individual brochures for a particular age group, call Waldorf Publications at 518-634-2222 and speak to Robin Bellack, or order online at www.waldorfpublications.org.

The Waldorf Kindergarten

The early years of childhood provide the foundation for a healthy life. Everything is important: the warmth of adults, the tone of voice, the aesthetics of the environment, to name a few aspects. This is the age when seeds are planted for a lifetime of adventure through learning. How this is brought to the child is crucial.

The following two essays by Waldorf educators provide a snapshot to help parents determine if this education is the appropriate one for their family. I say family because the two triangles of parent–child–teacher and home–classroom–professional educator should be in complete alignment.

What Young Children Really Need: The Essentials of Waldorf Early Childhood Education

by Susan Howard

Is there a Waldorf early childhood curriculum? Are there activities—puppet plays, circle games, watercolor painting, for example that are specific to a Waldorf program? Are there certain materials and furnishings—lazured, walls, handmade dolls, beeswax crayons, and other natural materials—that are necessary ingredients in a Waldorf setting? What makes Waldorf early childhood education Waldorf? Rudolf Steiner spoke on a number of occasions about the experiences that are essential for the healthy development of the young child.

These include:
- love and warmth
- an environment that nourishes the senses
- creative and artistic experiences

- meaningful adult activity to be imitated
- free, imaginative play
- protection for the forces of childhood
- gratitude, reverence, and wonder
- joy, humor, and happiness
- adult caregivers pursuing a path of inner development

Love and Warmth

Children who live in an atmosphere of love and warmth, and who have around them truly good examples to imitate, are living in their proper element.

– Rudolf Steiner, *The Education of the Child*

Love and emotional warmth, rather than any particular early childhood program, create the basis for the child's healthy development. These qualities should live between the adult caregiver and the child, in the children's behavior toward one another, and among the adults in the early childhood center. When Rudolf Steiner visited the classes of the first Waldorf school, he often asked the children, "Do you love your teacher?"

Children are also served if this love and warmth exist in the relationships between the teachers and the parents, between the early childhood teachers and the rest of the school, and in the surrounding community.

An Environment That Nourishes the Senses

The essential task of the kindergarten teacher is to create the proper physical environment around the children.

> The physical environment must be understood in the widest sense imaginable. It includes not just what happens around the children in the material sense, but everything that occurs in their environment, everything that can be perceived by their senses, that can work on the inner powers of the children from the surrounding physical space.
> – Rudolf Steiner, *The Education of the Child*

Early learning is profoundly connected to the child's own physical body and sensory experiences. Everything the young child sees, hears, and touches has an effect. Thus a clean, orderly, beautiful, quiet setting is essential.

The physical environment, both indoors and outdoors, should provide varied and nourishing opportunities for self-education experiences in touch, balance, lively and joyful movement, and also inward listening. The children should experience large-group, small-group, and solitary activities.

The teacher, in integrating diverse elements into a harmonious and meaningful environment, provides surroundings that are accessible to the child's understanding, feeling, and active will. The care, love, and intention expressed through the outer materials and furnishings of the classes are experienced unconsciously by the child. The child experiences the immediate environment as ensouled and nurturing.

The adult shapes the temporal environment as well as the spatial. Through a rhythmic schedule, in which the same thing happens at the same time on a daily, weekly, or monthly basis, the child gains a sense of security and confidence in the world. Also, the different activities of the day should take place in a comfortable flow with smooth transitions.

Creative, Artistic Experience

In order to become true educators, we must be able to see the truly aesthetic element in the work, to bring an artistic quality into our tasks. ... [If we bring this aesthetic element, then we begin to come closer to what the child wills out his own nature.

– Rudolf Steiner, *A Modern Art of Education*

In the early childhood classroom, the art of education is the art of living. The teacher is an artist in how she perceives and relates to the children and to the activities of daily life. She orchestrates and choreographs the rhythms of each day, each week, and each season in such a way that the children can breathe freely in a living structure.

In addition, the teacher offers the children opportunities for artistic experiences in singing and music, in movement and gesture—through eurythmy and rhythmic games—and in creative speech and language—through verses, poetry, and stories. The children model with beeswax, draw, and do watercolor painting. Puppet and marionette shows put on by the teacher are an important element in the life of the kindergarten.

Meaningful Adult Activity to Be Imitated

The task of the kindergarten teacher is to adapt the practical activities of daily life so that they are suitable for the child's imitation through play. ... The activities of children in kindergarten must be derived directly from life itself rather than being 'thought out' by the intellectualized culture of adults. In the kindergarten, the most important thing is to give children the opportunity to directly imitate life itself.

– Rudolf Steiner, *The Child's Changing Consciousness*

Real, meaningful work with a purpose, adjusted to the needs of the child, is in accordance with the child's natural and inborn need for movement and is an enormously significant educational activity. The teacher focuses on the meaningful activities that nurture life in the classroom 'home,' such as cooking and baking, gardening, doing laundry and cleaning, creating and caring for the materials in the immediate environment, and taking care of the bodily needs of the children.

This directed attention of the teacher creates an atmosphere of freedom in which the individuality of each child can be active. It is not intended that the children just copy the outer movements and actions of the adult, but that they experience also the inner attitude— the devotion, care, sense of purpose, focus, and creative spirit of the adult.

Free, Imaginative Play

In the child's play activity, we can only provide the conditions for education. What is gained through play, through everything that cannot be determined by fixed rules, stems fundamentally from the self activity of the child. The real educational value of play lives in the fact that we ignore our rules and regulations, our educational theory, and allow the child free rein.
— Rudolf Steiner, "Self Education in the Light of Spiritual Science"

Young children learn through play. They approach play in an entirely individual way, out of their unique configuration of soul and spirit, and out of their unique experiences of the world in which they live. The manner in which a child plays may offer a picture of how she will take up her destiny as an adult.

The task of the teacher is to create an environment that supports the possibility of healthy play. This environment includes the physical surroundings, furnishings, and play materials, the social environment of activities and social interactions, and the inner/spiritual environment of thoughts, intentions, and imaginations held by the adults.

Protection for the Forces of Childhood

>Although it is highly necessary that each person should be
>fully awake in later life, the child must be allowed to remain
>as long as possible in the peaceful, dreamlike condition
>of pictorial imagination in which his early years of life are
>passed. For if we allow his organism to grow strong in this
>nonintellectual way, he will rightly develop in later life the
>intellectuality needed in the world today.
>   – Rudolf Steiner, *A Modern Art of Education*

The lively, waking dream of the young child's consciousness must be allowed to thrive in the early childhood group. This means that the teacher refrains as much as possible from verbal instruction. Instead, her gestures and actions provide a model for the child's imitation. Familiar daily rhythms and activities provide a context in which the need for verbal instruction is reduced. Simple, archetypal imagery in stories, songs, and games provides experiences that the children can internalize but that do not require intellectual or critical reflection or explanation.

Gratitude, Reverence, and Wonder

>If, during the first period of life, we create an atmosphere
>of gratitude around the children, then out of this gratitude
>toward the world, toward the entire universe, and also out
>of thankfulness for being able to be in this world, a profound
>and warm sense of devotion will arise ... upright, honest,
>and true.
>   – Rudolf Steiner, *The Child's Changing Consciousness*

Early experience of gratitude is the basis for what will become a capacity for deep, intimate love and commitment in later life, for dedication and loyalty, for true admiration of others, for fervent spiritual or devotion, and for placing oneself wholeheartedly in the service of the world.

Joy, Humor, and Happiness

>If you make a surly face so that a child gets the impression
>you are a grumpy person, this harms the child for the rest

of his life. What kind of school plan you make is neither here
nor there; what matters is what sort of person you are.
– Rudolf Steiner, *The Kingdom of Childhood*

The teacher's earnestness about her work and her serious striving
must be balanced with humor and a demeanor that bespeaks
happiness. There must be moments of humor and delight in the
classroom every day.

Adult Caregivers on a Path of Inner Development
For the young child before the change of teeth, the most
important thing in education is the teacher's own being.
– Rudolf Steiner, *Essentials of Education*

Young children need time in nature to experience wonder
and joy there. Just think what feelings arise in the soul of the
early childhood educator who realizes: What I accomplish
with this child, I accomplish for the grown-up person in
his twenties. What matters is not so much a knowledge
of abstract educational principles or pedagogical rules. ...
[W]hat does matter is that a deep sense of responsibility
develops in our hearts and minds and affects our worldview
and the way we stand in life.
– Rudolf Steiner, "Education in the Face of the
Present-day World Situation"

Here we come to the spiritual environment of the early childhood
setting: the thoughts, attitudes, and imaginations living in the adult
who cares for the children. The invisible realm that lies behind the
outer actions of the teacher has a profound influence on the child's
development.

The spiritual environment includes recognition of the child as a
threefold being—of body, soul, and spirit—on a path of evolutionary
development through repeated Earth lives. This recognition provides
a foundation for the daily activities in the kindergarten and for the
relationship between adult and child.

Such an understanding of the nature and destiny of the human
being comes out of the inner life of the adult, the life of the individual

Ego. This is a realm that is largely hidden, and hence is difficult to observe directly and to evaluate objectively. Yet ultimately this realm may affect the development of the children most profoundly. It is not merely our outer activity that influences the growing child. What lies behind and is expressed through this outer activity is also crucial. Ultimately, the most profound influence on the child is who we are as human beings and who we are becoming and how.

Conclusion

The 'essentials' described here are qualitative in nature. For the most part, they are not part of a body of concrete 'best practices.' Instead, they concern inner qualities and attributes of the teacher that foster healthy development in young children. These qualities can come to expression in a wide variety of ways, according to the age range of the children in the group and their individual characteristics; the nature of the particular program—a kindergarten, playgroup, or extended care program; and the environment and surroundings— urban or rural, home or school or child care center.

Many practices that have come to be associated with Waldorf/ Steiner early childhood education— certain daily rhythms and rituals, play materials, songs, stories, even the colors of the walls, the dress of the adults, and the menu for snack—may be mistakenly taken as essentials. The results of such assumptions can be surprising, even disturbing—a 'King Winter' nature table appearing in a tropical climate in 'wintertime,' or dolls with pink skin and yellow hair in a kindergarten where all the children are brown-skinned and black-haired. Such practices may express a tendency toward a doctrinal or dogmatic approach that is out of touch with the realities of the immediate situation and instead imposes something from 'outside.' There is a parallel concern at the other end of the spectrum from the doctrinal or dogmatic. The freedom that Waldorf education offers each individual teacher to determine the practices of her early childhood program can be misinterpreted to mean that anything goes, according to personal preference and style. Here too, there is a danger that the developmental realities and needs of the children are not sufficiently taken into consideration. Each of these one-sided approaches may be injurious to the development of the children. As Waldorf early childhood educators, we are constantly seeking a middle, universally human path between polarities. Rudolf Steiner's advice to the first Waldorf kindergarten teacher, Elizabeth Grunelius, in the early 1920s, can be paraphrased as follows:

Observe the children.
Actively meditate.
Follow your intuitions.
Work so that all your actions are worthy of imitation.

Today, those of us who work with young children in a Waldorf environment are challenged to engage in a constant process of renewal. We must actively observe the children in our care, carry them in our meditations, and seek to work consciously and artistically to create the experiences that will serve their development. Our devotion to this task awakens us to the importance of self-education and transformation in the context of community. Our ongoing study of child and human development, our own artistic and meditative practices, and our work with anthroposophy, independently and together with others, become essential elements for the practice of Waldorf early childhood education. Here we can come to experience that we are not alone on this journey. We are supported through our encounters with one another and through our sharing of insights, experience, and knowledge. We are helped also by those spiritual beings who are committed to our continued development and to the renewal of culture that Waldorf education seeks to serve.

SUSAN HOWARD is the coordinator of the Waldorf Early Childhood Association of North America (WECAN). She is also active as a mentor and advisor to Waldorf kindergartens and as co-coordinator of the International Association for Steiner/Waldorf Early Childhood Education, based in Stockholm (www.iaswece.org). Susan lives in Amherst, Massachusetts, with her husband, Michael, an artist, writer, and adult educator.

Strengthening the Foundational Senses
of the Young Child

by Nancy Blanning and Laurie Clark

Many of us who work with young children have noticed that in recent years children have changed in ways that concern and alarm us. More children today are showing physical and social difficulties than we have seen in the past.

In preschools and kindergartens, many children, for example, are thin, pale, and chronically tired. They are nervous, cannot sit still, and are so fidgety that they often fall off their chairs. Movement and play do not come as easily as they once did. Many children are uncoordinated in their movements and seem clumsy. Some move with unconscious and uncontrolled abandon, smashing and crashing into their playmates. Others find a quiet corner and just stay there, avoiding movement at all cost. "Touchiness"—overreacting to the slightest brush against another child—emotional fragility, and difficulties with eating are also common. Many children reject the wholesome, simple foods that are prepared for snack and prefer instead only a few, often highly refined, foods.

Many young children also have trouble listening and processing what they hear. During circle time, the central event in the kindergarten

morning, they are distracted and have trouble imitating the teacher's gestures. And when during story time the children are offered nourishment of soul and spirit, some among them cannot inwardly create the mighty imaginative pictures contained in the stories.

Children generally also show an increased difficulty in interacting harmoniously with their classmates. The peaceful and healthy hum of free play that once characterized each day in the kindergarten is now difficult to create and sustain. In the past, children were more able to create play from their own imaginations. Now they imitate characters from the media. But the roles and the behaviors do not in fact relate to real human relationships, and conflicts and problems arise.

Taken together, these phenomena indicate that children are having difficulty in developing a healthy balance in body, mind, and soul through integration of the senses described above. They lack the basic sense of well-being and harmony in their physical bodies that should characterize a healthy childhood.

According to Rudolf Steiner, the human being has twelve senses. Four can be called the foundational senses. These are the sense of touch (the tactile sense); the sense of life; the sense of self-movement (the proprioceptive sense); and the sense of balance (the vestibular sense). It is by means of these that the soul and spirit of the child find their way into the structured physical body.

The **tactile sense** is the first to be awakened. This happens in the birth process itself when the mother's uterine contractions massage the fetus, giving it a first strong, external stimulus and awakening and toning the sense of touch. A very short labor, a Cesarean section, or a postpartum period spent in an incubator can result in an oversensitivity in the infant and young child. For this child, a normal tactile experience can be like an assault, and the child will avoid the exploration of the world through touch that is part of the development of the infant and toddler. He is often finicky about the fit of his clothes, about being touched, and about the temperature and textures of food.

Sometimes the tactile sense is overtaxed as in a long and stressful labor. Then the child's sense of touch closes down in a gesture of self-protection. This child can be unaware she has touched another child, that her hands are encrusted with sand and mud, or that her shoes are on the wrong feet. As Steiner points out, touch gives us an experience of our boundaries, telling us where we end and where the rest of the world begins. A healthy sense of touch lays the foundation for a sense of social boundaries.

The **sense of life** tells us whether our basic physiological processes, such as those involved in eating, sleeping, breathing, and eliminating waste products, are functioning properly. When things are going well, we are usually unaware of this sense and what it is monitoring. When there is a problem, the life sense creates the feeling of being out-of-sorts or unwell. Aches and pains, problems related to sleep and to waking up, to eating (indigestion, food allergies, inability to tolerate a variety of foods), register on the life sense. Predictable rhythm In daily life and warm interest from the child's caregiver support the life sense.

The **proprioceptive sense**, or sense of self-movement, tells us about the position and movement of our body. In each moment it informs us of the location in space of the head, trunk, and limbs and how they relate to each other. It does so by sensing the contraction and stretching of muscles and the compression of joints.

A child with a poorly developed proprioceptive sense may move through a room like a tornado, bumping into people and things. He may love to be at the bottom of a pile of other children. The external stimulus gives him the experience of body position and physical boundaries that his own proprioceptive sense fails to indicate. Such a child can be truly unaware of where his limbs are and how they are moving. He can be sincerely incredulous that with a swing of his arm he has just knocked down a block house that other children have spent twenty minutes building.

Healthy proprioception also provides the ability to begin a movement, to control it, and to stop it. This sense of self-movement enables us to maintain the right amount of muscle tension for a task such as lifting a glass of water. It also allows us to stand upright. A child with a poor sense of self-movement finds keeping an upright posture difficult and may collapse on the floor when the opportunity presents itself, as during circle time. A child, then, who is clumsy, who often bumps into things and other persons, and who readily slumps or just falls down, may have difficulty with the proprioceptive sense.

The **sense of balance**, or the vestibular sense, informs us of our position in space in relation to gravity. Working together with the proprioceptive sense, the sense of balance tells us where we are in relation to our surroundings and keeps us in balance, upright in space.

The vestibular sensory organs—the semicircular canals—are located in the inner ear. Ear infections, often chronic in nature, are very common among young children today, having replaced measles, chicken pox, and other inflammatory diseases that are now prevented by vaccines. Thus, both the vestibular sense and the sense of hearing are under attack. Some antibiotics used to fight ear infections may actually damage the inner ear and the semicircular canals.

Children with vestibular weakness are usually one of two extreme types. One type is very sensitive to movement of every sort and avoids spinning around, swinging, and being upside down. The other craves movement at all times. A child of this type can spin round and round on the tire swing and never get dizzy. She seems to need constant motion, always fidgeting and rocking in her chair. The vestibular sense in these children is underresponsive and thus needs a constant stream of stimuli to determine where the child's center of balance is. This child may also be the daredevil who lacks an appropriate sense of caution.

The importance of this sense of balance cannot be overemphasized. It is a unifying element in the whole system and seems to prime the entire nervous system to function properly.

The healthy development of these four senses in the young child provides the foundation for all the higher-level skills—cognitive, social, spiritual—in childhood and throughout life. When the foundational senses are functioning well, the child has pleasure and joy in being within his/her body. He moves in a balanced, coordinated, integrated way. He is eager to explore the world and new sensory experiences, and is not timid. The child is well-balanced, both literally and metaphorically, and also understands social boundaries.

In fact, however, many and increasing numbers of children lack the healthy development of these four senses. The incarnation into the physical body through the four foundational senses has been disrupted, and the harmony of young children's movement and behavior is disturbed. There are various explanations for this. Audrey McAllen, founder of the "The Extra Lesson," a method that is used widely in Waldorf schools for dealing with learning, behavioral, and other problems, cites the constant and powerful sensory stimulation to which today's children are subjected.

Well-known author Joseph Chilton Pearce elaborates this view by describing the "startle effect" and its use by the mass media. Pearce writes that children are essentially catatonic while watching television—and thus not really paying attention to the program or to the commercial breaks. Television producers therefore inject loud, unexpected, noises and sudden changes in volume and lighting into the programs to shock the child (and adult) back into an attentive state. These powerful stimuli cause the sympathetic nervous system to release an adrenal hormone usually secreted only in emergency situations. Cortisol quickens the heart and breathing rates, increases muscle tension, and prepares the child for fight or flight. Thus, children who spend time in front of a television are relentlessly bombarded with powerful sensory stimuli that keep them in a state of arousal. Music videos, movies, and computer games also contribute to this chronic overstimulation. Pearce sees media as one cause of the anxiety and sensory disorders that plague children today.

The extreme sensory stimulation a child encounters in electronic entertainment prepares him for a crisis situation in which responsive action is needed. Since no such situation ensues, the child's body begins to take a certain level of cortisol as normal. What once aroused the fight or flight response (and woke him up for the commercials) becomes inadequate. Thus, in recent years the creators of electronic entertainment have steadily increased the speed at which the images change, the volume of the sound effects, and the shock quality of the images themselves.

The lack of opportunities for movement, especially free, spontaneous physical movement, also affects children negatively. Rather than walking or riding a bicycle to school and to visit friends, children today are chauffeured here and there by parents. Because of safety concerns, children are unlikely to enjoy unsupervised play and exploration with friends in the neighborhood. They spend much time being entertained passively by television, movies, videos, and computers. Most are spared the daily chores and household tasks that in an earlier age trained and strengthened the foundational senses.

The daily activities in the Waldorf kindergarten all work to strengthen these primary senses. The periods of free play; the rhythmic games that involve clapping and stomping the feet and other bodily movements; the acting out in gesture of events in the stories told by the teacher; and the participation in the chores and household activities that take place in the kindergarten, such as sweeping, washing dishes, setting the table for snack, and kneading bread dough, all promote the child's coming into the physical body in a healthy way. Each of these elements in the daily sequence of activities is enhanced by the teacher's warm enthusiasm and by the beauty of the classroom.

Many kindergarten teachers augment these standard Waldorf activities with special movement experiences. These teachers have the children do a series of movements within an imaginative pictorial context. The imaginations give the movement a power and meaning and carry that movement deep into the child's being. These imaginatively enriched movements have a more profound effect than do straightforward calisthenics or physical therapy and can be therapeutic as well as hygienic.

For example, a kindergarten class might be told the story of "Tippery Tim and the Pot of Gold." Tippery Tim is a leprechaun who is guarding a pot of gold at the end of a rainbow. The class goes on a journey to find Tippery Tim. The children crawl under the roots of an imaginary tree to look for him, walk over a bridge (an elevated balance beam), run under a waterfall (a turning jump rope), and roll down from the top of the rainbow (do log rolls down gym mats arranged to create a small hill) before finally finding the gold. This is done each week over a term, and each week Tippery Tim has a small treasure in his gold pot for each child—a crystal, a star, and finally bells like the ones the leprechaun wears on the toes of his shoes.

There are things parents can do to help their children develop these foundational senses in a healthy way. These include:

* holding to a daily predictable rhythm and pattern that mealtimes, bedtime, and the times for other important daily activities are consistent;
* providing opportunities for free play and exploration indoors and out;
* taking children frequently and regularly for walks and outings in nature, regardless of the weather;
* encouraging the playing of games that involve running, jumping, skipping, balancing, crawling, and hopping (traditional children's games such as hide and seek, hop scotch, and jump rope are ideal);
* avoiding exposure to the media, particularly television, videos, and computers;
* encouraging children to eat a wide range of wholesome foods.

Today's culture is filled with threats to the healthy unfolding of the foundational senses in the young child. But if we are conscious of these hazards, we can nevertheless give our children a sound physical basis for life in the world and insure their development into healthy adults.

NANCY BLANNING is a retired kindergarten teacher after many years of teaching and remedial therapeutic work at the Denver Waldorf School, Colorado. Nancy is editor of Gateways, the WECAN newsletter.

LAURIE CLARK is the lead kindergarten teacher at the Denver Waldorf School where she has taught for over 30 years.

Waldorf: The Elementary Years

When you send your child(ren) to school, you are passing them over to an environment and individuals that will have a profound effect on them for the rest of their lives. In fact, during any given week of school, your children will be under this influence more than with you during their waking lives. It is here the seeds are planted for morality, love of learning, and social integration.

What are these seeds? How does environment affect child development? What subjects and skills should be taught in developmentally appropriate ways? How should school and home work together to the benefit of the children? What childhood activities promote healthy cognitive development so that learning becomes a lifelong passion?

This pamphlet contains four essays to help make informed decisions about whether Waldorf education is right for your family. Waldorf education is not an offshoot from the stream of education – it is its own stream from its own source.

You may follow up this short reading with other books from the bountiful collection from Waldorf Publications that can be found on the online bookstore at www.waldorfpublications.org. A highly recommended introductory view-book is *Windows into Waldorf*. You can view the results of studies of Waldorf graduates in the books: *Survey of Waldorf Graduates I* and especially *Survey of Waldorf Graduates II*.

Confronting the Culture of Disrespect

by Langdon Winner

Two features of contemporary American life may seem entirely unconnected, but upon closer inspection they stand out as dimensions of the same unsettling pattern. One is an all-too-familiar disposition in human relationships, an attitude about how to treat people that strongly affects our children and undermines even the best-planned attempts to educate them. Although it manifests itself in what seem to be scattered, annoying incidents in the lives of kids, this attitude has recently achieved attention as a malady of national concern. A second feature finds expression in a strategy of technological change characteristic of our dynamic "new economy." Celebrated as a wonderful recipe for prosperity, this strategy is rooted in a general orientation to the world that, in its broader dimensions, projects a dubious path for social development.

To introduce the phenomena, I would ask you to notice the bitter sting they bring to the lives of many children. We all know that teasing and bullying have long been problems in childhood and adolescence. Most of us have encountered such nastiness in one way or another; it's something many young people have always had to get used to, move beyond, and eventually outgrow. But during the past two decades or so, activities formerly dismissed as innocuous pestering have undergone a profound transformation. Tearing down people in public, making them feel bad about who they are and what they feel, has intensified and become a refined art, one supported by powerful forces in our culture.

The youngsters I know best are boys – my own children and their friends in middle school and high school – who put up with verbal abuse, subtle threats and put-downs in school every day. Some in the group are strong enough to withstand the continuous barrage, dishing it back or just ignoring the stupid, vicious taunts. But I've seen a number of boys wither under the barrage, fall silent, retreat into computer games, change schools, and disconnect from all but one or two friends who also feel abused by their classmates.

Teachers in both public and independent schools tell me that the atmosphere of negativity in student subcultures, far from being a minor annoyance, has become one of the most serious barriers to teaching and learning they have to confront each day, filling much of the social space in halls and classrooms. No one seems to know what to do about it. When I suggested to my wife, a counselor at an independent school, that we tackle the problem directly, at least among the boys and parents who are in our close circle of friends – have a meeting where a policy of "no tear down" would be discussed – she said it would not work,

that "kids don't operate that way." She's probably right. But what other solutions are available? There seem to be no ready answers.

It's clear that kids are busily at work sorting and sifting and categorizing: who's a jock, who's a prep, who's a nerd, who's a goth, who's located where in the pecking order. Generations of teenagers, including my own decades ago, have played this game, sometimes with appalling results. But somehow the persistence, intensity and sheer meanness of the process we see today goes much further. We know that Dylan Klebold and Eric Harris, the two killers at Columbine High School in Colorado, saw themselves as retaliating against schoolmates who had repeatedly tormented them. There is, of course, no excuse for their murderous acts. But what surprises me is how frequently I hear boys I know staunchly defend Klebold and Harris in words that come close to admiration. "Oh, yeah, I know where they were coming from," they observe without a hint of irony. "I have to put up with that stuff too."

The name I would give to the malady that afflicts young people is aggressive disrespect. In today's slang it is known as "dissing," an attitude brashly exhibited throughout our society. It's present in movies, television programs, radio talk shows, sports, journalism, and politics. In stand-up comedy and sit-coms, the prevalent form of humor is the put-down followed by a burst of canned laughter: insult – laugh track – public embarrassment – laugh track – personal barb – laugh track. It's also common in sports where trash talk and dissing have become essential rituals of the game. One also sees it in the personal attack ads that have become standard fare in election campaigns, a style of propaganda that allows candidates on both sides to avoid discussing important public issues and to blather on about an opponent's "character" instead.

In movies and television, of course, the relentless barrage of verbal abuse is tied to exhibitions of physical violence, where catharsis is achieved by shooting one's enemies, beating them up, or blowing them away. The same is true of video games – Quake, Doom, Half Life, and countless others – where the players participate in simulated gore. Earlier hopes that video games would engage children in more positive, educationally enriching activities have proven a risible fantasy. All of the best-selling games involve the players in ceaseless episodes of mayhem and slaughter. In all the electronic media available to them, our children receive a steady diet of social contempt produced by prominent role models encouraging aggressive disrespect, disrespect that assumes violence as its natural terminus. To an increasing extent this way of being is what is expected of young people, what is held out as "cool" in our society. Unlike the "cool" upheld by beatnik poets of the 1950s – existential detachment with Zen aspirations – today's "cool" is simply the meeting ground of unreflective nihilism and shopping mall fashion.

My point is not that television, video games and other forms of mass media "cause" the kinds of violence of the sort that crops up so often in American schools. It is always difficult to pinpoint specific causes of savagery within the complex strands of influence that shape people's behavior. What I want to point out instead are some astonishingly bleak background conditions that color the experiences and expectations of childhood in our time. In ways that our nation refuses to confront, the everyday sources of torment now undermine prospects for a healthy sense of self, crippling a youngster's ability to engage the world in active, hopeful ways. Struggling with the culture of contempt, boys – and many girls as well – learn to "be strong" by internalizing a distinctly dreary vision of life's possibilities.

The mood of aggressive disrespect is also prominent in what appears to be an entirely separate realm of human affairs, namely that of business and technology, celebrated as a place of lively entrepreneurship, innovation and productivity, supposedly the path to a brighter future. Here we see the glorious marriage of capital and technique spawning countless projects that will eventually alter how people live and think. The economic approach commonly followed in this domain at present is what the economist Joseph Schumpeter long ago called "creative destruction." As interpreted today, this means that one begins by locating an entity with recognized value attached to it, often a value that has existed in a particular social setting for a long while.

The challenge is to devise an alternative, an effective replacement launched in a new medium, especially the dynamic medium of digital communications. This strategy presents opportunities for rapid recapitalization and reorganization in every corner of economic life. Markets are captured and profits won as digital bits and money flow in new directions at the speed of light. In this process every institution, practice, relationship, artifact, and natural entity is now subject to renovation and/or replacement. The fact that an object, activity or institution has flourished for decades and has tangible value attached to it is sufficient grounds for targeting it for liquidation. In the global marketplace, if an entity cannot compete with the alternatives arrayed against it, then it is doomed to extinction.

An example of what I am calling aggressive disrespect here is exhibited in Daniel Burrus' book *Technotrends*. Burrus argues that if your line of work has become what he calls a "cash cow," a reliable source of income, you must innovate in ways that replace it with the newest, relevant technology. "Kill your cash cow or someone will do it for you," Burrus advises. In this way of thinking, for example, teachers would be well-advised to get out of the teaching business and into educational software because that is where the technotrends are moving. The prescription: liquidate all sources of value and re-capitalize.

An outlook of this sort is coin of the realm in Silicon Valley, Seattle, and other centers of high tech panache. To suggest that an organism, artifact, or institution should be acknowledged for what it is, respected or even cherished for the good it does, is entirely at odds with this sensibility. Tools, traditions, and whole biological genomes are now under scrutiny for the ways in which they might be altered or replaced by those with better, profit-seeking plans.

To ask respect for any person, thing, practice, or institution is problematic because, as we all know, respect is something that must be earned. But if one lives in a culture that relishes disrespect for anything and everything, then teachable moments about how things earn enduring value are few and far between. Even the earlier sense that there was an overall, accumulated residue of scientific, technical and social change that could reasonably be called "progress" is no longer a topic of interest. Only those changes predicated on a limited, short-term, rapid turnover of goods are ones worth considering. That is why so many people prefer the terms "innovation" and "creative destruction" to the outmoded category of "progress" these days.

The various kinds of aggressive disrespect I've described are clearly connected in important ways. For example, if one wanted a society in which students would leave schools highly dissatisfied and disrespectful of anything in society and nature, ready to launch changes for the sake of change itself, then the schools we've got are serving quite well, for they operate as laboratories of disrespect and breeding grounds for restless innovation without any deeper human purpose. Students leave the schools ready for the mentality of high tech enterprise – the belief that everything that exists is simply an opportunity for innovation and profitable reconfiguration. Books, libraries, bookstores, publishers – throw them out and begin anew. Teachers, classrooms, conventional teaching materials – discard them and start over with online gadgets.

Here's the prescription for change: Identify any vocation or profession – find a way to re-encode its message; take it to the market; cash in your stock options and move on to the next golden opportunity. It works just as well with objects in nature. Take the genome of a fruit fly (or what we're told is its close relative, the human being). Uncover its genetic map and get ready to move and shake.

Among engineers and technical experts there has long been earnest discussion about the ethics that ought to guide professional conduct. Over many decades a wide range of moral principles and arguments has helped focus reflection on this matter. But increasingly, it seems to me, there is a de facto ethic that guides what a great many people are inclined to do in matters of technological change. It is the ethic of "Hell, why not?" A restlessness and dissatisfaction continually seek opportunities to modify whatever entities seem ripe for transformation and recapitalization. That disposition toward change is far different from the one that seeks positive, lasting improvement in society, in our relations with natural things, or in the artificial complex that surrounds us. No, that is simply not what technical intentions are about these days.

It is with considerable grief that I recall the kinds of overt and quiet suffering I've witnessed among the youngsters assaulted by the culture of disrespect and pressured to join it. As people, things, and ideas are dissed, dismantled, demolished, and discarded, what can be done to help them? What can protect them from the ways of being so persuasively modeled? What can deflect them from the work of callous disrespect that awaits them within today's hyperlinked, hyperventilating corporate economy?

I don't know. But pondering the torrents of disrespect I've seen drowning the spark of childhood recently, I'm reminded of a letter Henry James once sent to a nephew who had asked his advice on how to succeed. James decided to give the young man some simple wisdom:

Three things in human life are important.
The first is to be kind.
The second is to be kind.
And the third is to be kind.

I wonder: In a period of history hell-bent on other pursuits, how can the virtues of kindness and respect toward other beings be taught?

LANGDON WINNER is Professor of Political Science in the Department of Science and Technology Studies at Rensselaer Polytechnic Institute. He is author of two classic studies of technology and its impact on modern culture, Autonomous Technology and The Whale and the Reactor: A Search for Limits in an Age of High Technology.

"Teaching" Morality – Is It Possible?
Uncovering the Small Still Voice Within

by Patrice Maynard

A generation ago, in the children's magazine called *Highlights for Children*, every issue had, in addition to stories, activities, and crafts, a regular feature called "Goofus and Gallant." These names of two brothers always proved prophetic. Goofus always did the wrong, impolite, or uncivic thing while his brother, Gallant, by contrast always did the right, kind, moral thing. This section was one of my favorites because, even at the ripe old age of nine, these little vignettes struck me as hilarious. As Gallant held the door for people and Goofus slammed the same door on others, the contrast was made funny to me because somehow it was obvious that if someone were depraved enough to actually make the choices Goofus made, he would not be aware of the mistake, and would not be moved to change his habits because of the "Goofus and Gallant" section of this magazine. If someone on staff at *Highlights* felt that writing "Goofus and Gallant" was a good way to teach morality, children knew better. Already having an innate sense of rightness, my heart knew that this way of showing right and wrong was more humorous than helpful.

My reaction as a nine-year-old to "Goofus and Gallant" could be named "youthful cynicism." Cynicism is the result whenever the

teaching of morality or right and wrong in behavior is overdone. Any lecturing seventh grade teacher knows this. Preaching incites cynicism. Every heart and soul has in it a "small still voice" which knows the truth and advises our actions. To lecture to this innate sense of truth and morality is to insult its owner into feeling untrusted and unrecognized. When the call goes in trust to this "small still voice within" a human consciousness, especially in the young, when the one who calls is a teacher, a beloved adult, the response is relief in the child. The child is recognized as moral and so responds with happiness to such a call with this "small still voice of truth within."

In Waldorf schools, this practice of recognition and calling to prompt a response from a quiet voice deep within the child is used daily by Waldorf teachers. The following describes three tools used to do just this effectively.

Effective Tool #1 for Encouraging Morality in Children: The Story

Stories fill the curriculum of the elementary grades in every Waldorf school. Waldorf teachers search for and invent stories that have inherent in them a quality of transformation. All true fairy tales, to offer examples from a classical story form, have in them moments when swans are returned to their forms as human beings, the youngest brother unexpectedly wins the princess, or Snow White awakens from death-like sleep. Teachers understand that children know in their hearts that this transformation is their most precious capacity as human beings: the power to do something right or wrong and the strength needed to make right what has been done wrong. Every time a child listens to a story, the capacity to think clearly about rightness and wrongness is exercised.

It has always astonished me, while teaching in a Waldorf school, how children know – in every story – when something is about to go wrong. We all love stories, children most especially, and we will go to great lengths to hear a story. The most rambunctious children will sit quietly in the hope of hearing a story. This element of transformation lifts up hearts and offers instruction in how to change, to correct things, and to strive. As a class teacher in a Waldorf school, one learns to use these constants in children's aspirations, to become an adept storyteller.

Any skilled teller of tales will explain that it is essential to anticipate those parts in each story that will rouse the listener to inner reaction. In every tale of transformation there is a moment, a critical action, that causes everything to go terribly wrong. All children recognize these moments instantly, without fail. A classroom full of first graders can become electrifyingly quiet when, for example, in "The Nixie of the Mill Pond," a Grimms' tale, the Nixie guarantees to make the Miller, whose prosperity has dwindled, rich as a king if he will only promise her the first-born thing he finds when he returns home. There is at this moment in the storytelling an inevitable intake of breath that can be heard throughout the classroom. All the children's little faces express the same thing: "No. Don't do it. There's something wrong with a bargain like this." They are, of course, right. In his desperation for wealth, the Miller speculates that it could be nothing more than a kitten or a puppy. He agrees to the Nixie's plan but finds, on returning home, that he has promised the Nixie his newborn son. A mixture of anxiety and hope then rises as a mood in the class from the thinking hearts of the children. What will the Miller do to redeem what he has done? Consider some of the many moral issues for a child to ponder in such a moment in a story: Greed dims clear thinking; some deeds have dire consequences; bargaining with living things is not a good idea; and seductive forces should not be succumbed to quickly.

More important than speculating on the mystery of how children can recognize these moments so consistently is the observation that children grow strong in moral judgment when they have the chance to practice the measuring of right and wrong inwardly in the course of their days. Stories offer abundant opportunities. Up through the grades, through tales of Aesop, tales of mythology, tales of the lives of great men and women, stories of alchemists who forged the science of chemistry, and stories of the Earth and its mountains and waterways – all give the growing human being a chance to exercise his or her moral muscle.

Effective Tool #2 for Encouraging Morality in Children: The Truth Offered in the Experience of the World

Anyone who has had the good fortune to sing in a choir or a chorus knows that when there is consensus on a tone and everyone recognizes this, a larger experience of the tone occurs to everyone singing it and the tone is enhanced, deepened, enriched. Like the "zone" of a runner, this is an experience that lifts the singers out of the ordinary time-space continuum.

Painters will explain that when a color or a mix of colors on a canvas or paper is clean, unclouded by accidental or poor mixing, the result on the surface being painted has the same quality as the single tone from many voices. The painter's heart follows the color, knows what to paint next, and is at peace.

Sculptors in wood, when they have acclimated to the piece of wood they use, describe a similar "zone" of being one with the wood and knowing which pieces to chip away. They go with the wood and attain a "zone" of steady work and the loss of a sense of time in the satisfying feeling of comprehending the wooden substance.

Each of the artists delineated above experiences the truth of the artistic work undertaken. The artist comprehends "rightness" in tone, color, or wood and feels satisfaction in this experience of correctness.

In Waldorf schools, all children digest all subject matter artistically. Children paint, draw, sing, play musical instruments, knit, sew, embroider, weave, sculpt, carve, work metal, dance, and strive for grace in athletics. They do all this not to prepare to be artists, as some who do not understand Waldorf education are misled to believe. There are many reasons behind this approach to a curriculum. For our purposes here, it is to strengthen the moral intuition of the developing human being. In the arena of artistic work, there are no formulas to lead to success or to something beautiful. The one engaged in the artistic activity, whatever it may be, must know when something is "right" or "complete." A soul that has struggled artistically is strong in the sense of right and wrong. This artistic sensibility is directly transferable to the many decisions in life about friends and family, acts of kindness, civic responsiveness, and situations holding moral dilemmas. The "muscle" exercised is that of a sense of truth, rightness, completeness.

In addition to the cultivation of moral sensibilities through this experience of a "zone" of correctness through artistic work, a student experiences profound truth in using the materials of the Earth for artistic pursuits. Pure color, pure tone, the grain of wood, the warmth of wool, the movement of the well-designed human body – all have in them truth and beauty. The child, the student learns the truth inherent in the substances of the Earth by using them, handling them, finding the possibilities and limitations in them. In successful artistic work, finding the rightness of the substance and transforming it into something designed by the artist honor the truth of the substance and the will of the artist. Something beyond the artist is made and the artist grows.

Cultivating the wish to make something beautiful schools the soul, heart, thinking and will of a child to go beyond the self, honoring the substance and the world that will view the artistic piece. Artistic work also builds sensory skill and integration, making the elegant tools of sensory perception built into the wisdom of the human form the highest and best they can be through practice.

Again, these skills are transferable to life situations. A student who has the use of artistic capacities built through daily practice, not for becoming an artist but as a means of comprehension, works in all situations in life to comprehend the truth beyond the individual and the obvious, to make the world as beautiful as one can make it, and to experience all things completely. These are moral skills.

Effective Tool #3 for Encouraging Morality in Children: The Admiration and Emulation of Moral People

The most potent tool for calling children to moral activity is the last addressed here. After all is examined and evaluated, the goodness of teachers who stand before the children is the most powerful influence on the moral development of the young. Most educational thought in the current moment is focused on content and testing. In Waldorf schools teachers take up their own self-development with vigor because this work on self-transformation is the most powerful tool available to shape a lesson, a class, a young human being. Discipline is most effective in the presence of the self-disciplined. Children who work, play and live around adults who work assiduously on themselves will inwardly imitate, emulate, and aspire to do the same. In the words of Dr. Rudolf Steiner, whose  philosophy and educational ideals are the teachers of all Waldorf teachers, "It is not so much what you teach but who you are that matters."

In a culture preoccupied with material proof of reality, this last is the easiest to forget or to dismiss. Content and testing results usurp the attention of teachers whose vocational task is to encourage children to love the world and participate in it. Young people need adults to forge the way for them on the path of life. Teachers give children models of self-discipline and the practice of truth.

Teaching morality is entirely possible but not in the ways commonly thought. Stories full of powerful, beautiful images build a child's imagination. Artistic practice in digesting the experiences of the world builds a child's idealism to inspiration and a yearning to make the world more beautiful. Moral adults, who work on inner strength and self-development, give children these activities of self-discipline and self-development to emulate. As young people emulate they build their intuition and sense the rightness and beauty of the world. Calling to the child's heart in these ways to allow the inner voice, so tender and quiet, to speak in its simple sense of goodness, engages his or her aspirations to strive to be good, and the world changes for the better with this individual striving.

PATRICE MAYNARD is Director of Publications for Waldorf Publications at the Research Institute for Waldorf Education. She is a seasoned teacher, an officer in CAPE (Council for American Private Education located in Washington, DC) and an acclaimed lecturer.

Science and the Child

by Steve Talbott

Why do leaves turn red? Where does the sun go at night?
What made Whiskers, our cat, die? Will Mommy die
sometime, and, Daddy, will you die, too?

Children are notorious for posing naïve and perplexing questions. When one of our sons was four years old, he asked, "Why did God make poisonous snakes?" I do not recall our answer, but I very much doubt that it was helpful. And who among us can do justice to the most perplexing questions of all – the ones incarnated in every newborn child – Who are you, and for what purpose have you entered our lives?"

The child's large and difficult questions arise not from complex theoretical constructions, but from simplicity, "childish simplicity" we are tempted to say, with a slightly patronizing smile. We need, after all, to defend serious discourse against fruitless inquiries about God and the moral significance of poisonous snakes. This is why our more childlike questions have, over the past few hundred years, disappeared from science. They are anachronisms, echoing hollowly off the instrument panels and surgically precise tools of the laboratory. Their implications would be only an embarrassing distraction oddly disjoined from the prevailing paths of technical investigation. "Child, for what purpose have you come?" Imagine a genetic engineer or an evolutionary theorist asking such a question!

Yet a strange thing is happening. Questions rather like the child's impossible ones are now being forced upon us from the side of science. The biotechnologist, faced not with poisonous snakes but with "defective" children, is led to ask, "Where do these defects come from? Can we unmake them?" And further, regarding the child's destiny: "Why do we age and die? Must we submit passively to human limitation?"

I say "rather like" the child's questions. For the child is always inquiring about meaning and purpose. His question about why we age and die is morally, teleologically, and aesthetically tinged. The scientist, by contrast, is asking about the mechanisms that "implement" aging and death and wondering to what effect we might manipulate them.

Such, at least, is the usual distinction, not only between child and scientist, but also between the scientific dialogue and the larger human conversation. But the distinction is muddied when scientists tell us (or conspire in our belief) that they are gaining the knowledge to engineer better children. How can you recognize a better child if you must shun the language of value? More specifically, how can we, as scientists or parents, propose to manipulate an individual child's destiny if we cannot seriously ask about that destiny – about identity and purpose and tasks?

If the scientist is to join in such a conversation, then nothing less than a second scientific revolution will have occurred. Science will have been reopened to the categories of meaning, value, and purpose. The genetic engineer and the evolutionary theorist will learn to ask, "Child, for what purpose have you come and how can we make things better for you?"

Without such a revolution there will be no true societal conversation. Rather, we will hear two utterly different and dissonant styles of speaking, and they will spawn endless confusions between them. Using one style we will converse with the child, and therefore at least partly in the child's terms. With the other we will converse about the child, concerning ourselves with the manipulation of genetic, hormonal, neural, and other mechanisms as if we were engaged in little more than an engineering project.

Ends and Means

The President's Council on Bioethics, with its discussion of "Better Children," has stepped boldly into the no-man's land between these two ways of speaking. Perhaps wisely, "Beyond Therapy" has not asked for a revolution in science. Instead it has tried only to delimit the

engineering project and to establish the propriety of discussing the ends and purposes of human life.

The Council begins with the most fundamental question of all: "What, exactly, is a good or a better child?" Is it a child who is more able and talented? If so, able in what and talented how? Is it a child with better character? If so, having which traits or virtues? More obedient or more independent? More sensitive or more enduring? More daring or more measured? Better behaved or more assertive? Is it a child with the right attitude and disposition toward the world? If so, should he or she tend more toward reverence or skepticism, high-mindedness or toleration, the love of justice or the love of mercy? As these questions make clear, human goods and good humans come in many forms, and the various goods and virtues are often in tension with one another. Should we therefore aim at balanced and "well-rounded" children, or should we aim also or instead at genuine excellence in some one or a few dimensions?

Against the backdrop of these unanswered (and perhaps unanswerable) questions, the Council considers various genetic and pharmacological technologies that promise to give us "better" children. The first set of technologies aims at shaping, choosing, or improving a child's native endowments. Prenatal diagnosis permits us to weed out fetuses with undesirable genetic traits. Preimplantation genetic screening allows us to select in vitro embryos with desired genetic traits. Genetic engineering would allow us to produce certain genetic traits by deliberate design.

For now, prenatal diagnosis and preimplantation screening present only restricted possibilities for "improved" children. These methods are limited by the genetic resources of the parents, neither of whom may have the desired trait. Further, most traits require the interplay of many genes, so even if the parents had the right genes, it would be nearly impossible – short of producing and screening thousands of embryos – to find one with the right genetic combination. And even if our scientific understanding enabled us to identify trait-specific gene combinations reliably, it remains the case that our powers of control would still be limited. As the Council points out, "Since most traits of interest to parents seeking better children are heavily influenced by the environment, even successful genetic screening and embryo selection might not, in many cases, produce the desired result."

As for genetic engineering – that is, the direct insertion of desired genes into an embryo – the difficulties are even more imposing. Not only is there the challenge of working with genes that interact in still largely unknown ways, but there is also the problem of inserting these genes into the embryo without damaging it or causing unintended side-effects. The history of genetic engineering in nonhuman species has been one long crescendo of discovery about such unintended consequences.

The root of the problem is that the side-effects are not really side-effects. They are a meaningful activity of the organism. As Craig Holdrege has shown in *Genetics and the Manipulation of Life*, the organism deals with a genetic or biochemical intrusion much as it deals with a disturbance of its external environment – by responding as an integral whole. This is true even in the plant. For example, when researchers inserted carotene-producing genes in tomato plants, the plants did produce more carotene. But the substance appeared in plant parts that normally don't have carotene (seed coats and cotyledons) – and the more the carotene, the smaller the plant became. Similarly, when herbicide resistance was genetically engineered into a mustard species (Arabidopsis), the generally self-pollinating plants started cross-pollinating at twenty times the normal rate. Such side-effects, whether obvious or subtle, turn out to be more the rule than the exception.

The reason for this is simply that the organism adapts to a disturbance with its entire being and according to its own distinctive manner of existence. Manipulating the parts forces a question that can be answered only by the governing whole: "Who are you? What sort of a unity are you trying to express?" Even when our aim is nothing more than effective, machine-like control, we cannot prevent the organism from responding in a meaningful and conversational manner. And if this is the case with a plant, it is certainly also the case with a child.

Given the difficulties and limitations involved in the various genetic technologies, the Council believes that "prophecies and predictions of a 'new (positive) eugenics' seem greatly exaggerated." But this does not relieve it of concern about the changes now afoot. Even prenatal screening for disease, already a common practice, may be "shifting parental and societal attitudes toward prospective children: from simple acceptance to judgment and control, from seeing a child as an unconditionally welcome gift to seeing him as a conditionally acceptable product."

Beyond Passive-Aggressive Objectivity

In the second part of the chapter on "Better Children," the Council explores new pharmacological ways of altering children's behavior. It endorses the therapeutic use of behavior-modifying drugs in difficult cases, while questioning the casual reliance on drugs as a general strategy for obtaining well-balanced children. It notes that "most children whose behavior is restless and unruly could (and eventually do) learn to behave better, through instruction and example, and by maturing over time." Drugs short-circuit this learning process by acting directly on the body. They raise the question of whether we are looking for the mere outward, behavioral result, or, instead, for the inner shaping of character that can only be learned.

If the development of character depends on effort to choose and act appropriately, often in the face of resisting desires and impulses, then the more direct pharmacological approach bypasses a crucial element. The beneficiaries of drug-induced good conduct may not really be learning self-control; they may be learning to think it is not necessary. The child, that is, may come to "look upon himself as governed largely by chemical impulses and not by moral decisions grounded in some sense of what is right and appropriate."

So the control of behavior is one thing, and the moral education of the child is quite another. Given where we are now, making this distinction is an important step. But we should not imagine (and I doubt the Council imagines) that we have harmonized the two conversations. The dilemma remains: How do we bring the researcher's language of fact and control into worthwhile dialogue with the parent's language of ethics and purpose? Wouldn't this be like bringing the sober, sophisticated world of the mature scientist into meaningful relationship with the naïve, morally infused world of the child?

The idea of any such convergence may seem outrageous. And yet, when the scientist offers the parent a menu of options for obtaining "better children," it is he himself who puts the questions of meaning, value, and purpose on the table. When the going gets tough, he cannot fairly retreat into the "silence of objectivity." He cannot reasonably say, "I offer you better children, but do not ask me what 'better' means or who the child is." This passive-aggressive refusal to engage the issue is least acceptable when coming from the person who forced the issue in the first place – even if the issue threatens revolution.

Can We Get from "Ought" to "Is"?

In the blithe spirit of the child – whose destiny we are, after all, presuming to address – I wish to say a few words about the revolution. Desperately brief words, necessarily, but words suggestive, I hope, of an ultimate potential for our two conversations to become one.

Not that we should underestimate the challenge. Scientists have apparent reason for their reluctance to "come out of the closet" with

their values. It has long been part of their discipline to refuse as best they can all explicit dealings with questions of value, and the practical benefits of this austere objectivity appear to have been spectacular. In this light, the latter-day quandaries of biotechnology look suspiciously like a trap, baited with all those metaphysical and discipline-sapping enticements from which scientists have till now taken such great pains to flee. How, then, can we possibly ask the scientist, as a scientist, to participate in discussions about the moral education of the child or the moral implications of a genetic alteration? Don't we leave those topics for the ethicist?

More and more we do (as the President's Council on Bioethics can surely testify), which helps to explain the disjointed nature of the two conversations. The disjunction has long been canonized in the philosophical proverb, "You cannot get from facts to values." There is no way to get from statements about what is to statements about what ought to be. "Is" and "ought" seem to come from different, incommensurable worlds. It hardly needs adding that the scientist is passionately committed to the factual and objective – to the is-ness of things.

Look at the world through more childlike eyes, however, and the situation is wondrously transformed. The question becomes not how do we get from an "is" to an "ought," but rather the reverse. Putting it broadly: How do we manage to narrow our understanding down to a mere statement of fact when we start with such valuative and psyche-laden terms as "good," "evil," "ugly," "beautiful," "meaningful," and "purposeful"?

For we do start that way. Historically, the narrowing down is exactly what happened. By all accounts the ancients experienced themselves as living within an ensouled world – one thoroughly drenched in perceptions of goodness and value. Even the physis or "elementary substance" of the early Greek philosophers was, as Francis Cornford remarked, not only a material thing but at the same time a "soul-substance." Further, "the properties of immutability and impenetrability ascribed [by some Greek philosophers] to atoms are the last degenerate forms of divine attributes."

What is true historically is true also of the individual biography. The child, too, lives in an ensouled world. His incessant questions of meaning and purpose ("Why ...?") testify to an inborn conviction that the underlying reality of the world is psychic and voluntary, bearing an obligation to sustain good and reasonable appearances. Only with maturation does the child slowly gain a world of fact, an is-world, to set beside his birthright-world of congenial value.

Moreover, the birthright is never relinquished. Look at the mature human being – in the life of family and community, of work and recreation, of friendship and enmity, of politics and the academy – and you will be hard put to find a single act, word, or gesture that is not suffused with value and purpose. This is true even of the scientist in his laboratory, who, if he could really drain all his actions of their valuative content – say, by treating his colleagues like objects or, for that matter, treating sophisticated instruments like junk – would be dismissed as a psychopath.

No, we do not find a realm of value-free, psychically disinfected fact within the human sphere – except in one place: the intellectual constructions we have lately undertaken in the name of science and its philosophy. These constructions are aimed, as far as possible, at representing an antiseptic world cleansed of everything human. It has, of course, been doubted whether such a cleansing is possible. In any case – and speaking from the naïve, child-like vantage point – we might naturally paraphrase Cornford by asking whether the antiseptic world of mere fact is the last "degenerate" form of the psyche's intrinsically much fuller affirmations. Certainly this is the way it looks historically. But there is a further question of whether, even as a final achievement, the fact-world attains independence. Or does it remain parasitic upon the less denatured reality from which it arose?

Don't forget that these intellectual constructions of science take place according to certain restrictive rules, and the historical acceptance of the restrictions was a matter of choice. Moreover, the choices amounted to a decision, conscious or otherwise, to exclude from consideration everything meaningful and psyche-laden – everything that did not serve the insistent drive toward a pure is-world. And it remains highly significant that these very same choices are linked to the most problematic aspects of science today. Here are two examples of what I mean.

Focusing Down to a Null Point

The child who asks about the red leaves of autumn is asking about red, not the wavelengths and frequencies of a physics text. He lives within a vivid world of sense qualities. This is why the Dutch psychologist, Jan Hendrik van den Berg, conceived the following exchange:

"Why are the leaves red, Dad?"

"Because it is so beautiful, child. Don't you see how beautiful it is, all these autumn colors? That is how the leaves are red." There is no truer answer.

Of course, this is not the final or complete answer. As the child gets older, the answer could be enriched, not diminished, by an understanding of the interworkings and so-called "mechanisms" of a natural world that remains qualitative through and through. But a fateful choice intervened to alter any such understanding.

Beginning with Galileo there was a conscious disregard of qualities within science – and this for the simple reason that qualities, as every child knows, are inescapably freighted with psyche. We experience qualities "in here" – within consciousness. But what is insufficiently realized is that we also experience qualities "out there," in the only external world we have. We cannot characterize a world – any sort of world – without qualities. Subtract all qualitative content from your thoughts about things, and there will be no things left. Try to imagine a tree without color or visible form, without sound in a breeze, without the smell of sap and leaf, without felt solidity, and the tree will have ceased betraying any sign of its existence. If you are inclined to redeem the situation with talk of molecules or subatomic particles, try to characterize those without appealing to qualities!

It's fine to say, "We get from the qualitative world to the realities of hard science by dealing only with what can be quantified." But the phrase "what can be quantified" is puzzling, since it has no meaning if we cannot say anything significant about the "what" we are quantifying. Given a set of quantities, we have to know what they are quantities of, if we are to know anything at all about the actually existent world. And how do we characterize a "what" without qualities?

You can, then, begin to see what a vanishing, ghostly world we bequeath to the child. But, of course, scientists do in fact rely on their awareness of qualities. Otherwise, the world would have completely disappeared and they would have nothing to explain. It's just that the discipline of their science does not explicitly recognize the sense world in its own terms – the qualitative terms that pose not only the child's questions, but also the only questions a truly observation-based science can have. The reason for the omission is clear: If researchers actually reckoned with the qualities they begin with and rely on, they would no longer find themselves theorizing within a pure is-world. This by their own admission, since the whole reason for rejecting qualities in the first place is that they are "contaminated" by the psyche and its values.

A second historical choice, less conscious in its origins, was to proceed by a method of analysis, assigning ultimate explanatory significance to the furthest products of the analysis. The problem here is that one never stops to consider a thing in its own terms. The fiery tree of autumn resolves into root, branch, and leaf, the leaf into cells, the cells into organelles, the organelles into biochemicals ... and so on without end, down to the most remote, subatomic entities. "Without end" because there could be no satisfactory end. If understanding must be given in terms of analysis, and if the analysis were ever to stop at some fundamental, unanalyzable thing, then that thing (upon which all else is erected) must, according to our method, stand as an incomprehensible mystery, no more approachable than divine fiat.

Analysis is an essential direction of movement in all scientific cognition. But if it is not counterbalanced by an opposite movement, then we can never say anything about what is there – what is presenting itself significantly as this particular thing of this particular sort. We can speak only of the elements it consists of. But this hardly helps, for of these elements in their own right we can again say nothing, but must refer instead to what they consist of. We have no place to stop and say, "Behold this." By itself alone, the method is a way of never having to face anything. No wonder, then, that neither the evolutionary theorist nor the geneticist ever sees in the organism a creature of which we might stop and ask, "Who are you?"

A one-sided method of analysis, in other words, brings us again to a kind of emptiness. And, again, we must say: Science is not really empty. The scientist is always recognizing the insistent presence of things in the world – significant wholes – even if the nature of this recognition receives no formal or systematic acknowledgment alongside the analytic cleaving of wholes into parts. After all, you are not likely to set about analyzing a thing if you have not first glimpsed it, at least intuitively, as a significant entity in itself. But your preferred method of analysis does not encourage you to attend to this whole in its own terms. If it did, you might find yourself caught up in something more like a conversation than in the mere manipulation of parts.

A Little Child Shall Lead Them

These historical choices – to reject qualities and to proceed with a one-sided method of analysis – confront scientists with a problem that looms so threateningly near and so incomprehensibly large that ignoring it is almost the only option. If, however, we could get up the courage to face the problem squarely, it might suggest to us that we can never shrink the child's rich cognitive inheritance all the way down to an is-world of mere fact. We can approach this end-point only in modern physics, and we achieve the approach only by depriving our theoretical constructions of their content. The reassuring certainties we enjoy in these constructions are the formal certainties of mathematics. But they alone cannot give us a world. Some of the greatest physicists, in their more child-like, soul-searching moments, have admitted as much. Einstein once remarked: "As far as the propositions of mathematics refer to reality, they are not certain; and as far as they are certain, they do not refer to reality."

Another physicist, Sir Arthur Eddington, may have had the same problem in mind when he wrote:

> [Our knowledge of physics] is only an empty shell – a form of symbols. It is knowledge of structural form, and not knowledge of content. All through the physical world runs that unknown content, which must surely be the stuff of our consciousness.

Likewise, a preeminent physicist of our own era, Richard Feynman, confessed that "we have no knowledge of what energy is" – and this same cognitive darkness overshadows the other key terms of our physics, such as mass, force, motion, time, and space.

All this forcibly brings the truth home to us: We can hardly claim to have an is-world of fact without value, of object without subject, given that both fact and object have become blanks to us, with their content shoved under our methodological rug. Did we not exclude their content from view precisely because it speaks a language akin to our own interior? So, yes, if we ignore the world's content, we do come nearer to an is-world, but it turns out to be an empty world precisely because we have ignored its content. And this content is exactly what the child sees and puts a name to with his wonderfully innocent and simple observations.

You may think it strange to arrive at puzzles of physics in a discussion of biotechnology and its application to children. How have we gotten so far afield? But in an analytic era with its inevitable fragmentation and intense specialization, recovering a single, unified language for approaching the child means realizing first of all that far afield is not really far afield. The most fateful, scientifically developed "drug" we administer to the child is not some highly specialized biomolecule bathing his neurons, but rather the ambient, scientific worldview saturating his consciousness. And the whole effect of this view, centered as it is in the emptied fact-world of physics, is to rob nature of any congenial content for the child.

One way or another, we conduct a wide-ranging and gravely significant conversation with every child. If our language remains that of fact and control, then the language itself will dehumanize the child fully as much as any of the biochemical and genetic ministrations that are such natural consequences of the language.

In "Beyond Therapy" the President's Council on Bioethics has shown how revealing a second, value-centered language can be. But the decisive question remains whether we can bring the two ways of speaking together in a harmony of meaning. Can we, for example, learn to approach the genome in the spirit of the child's soul-piercing "Why ... ?" or the parent's quizzical "Who are you?" Might it be that real breakthroughs in genetics – breakthroughs of understanding rather than of technique – await our ability to look at the organism qualitatively, in its own meaningful terms? And if we do so, will we not find the whole speaking through every part, so that the child's genome can, when approached in the right spirit, be discovered as part of the child's – this child's – revelation of himself? Finally, is not our receptivity to this revelatory aspect of the human organism a prerequisite for entering into a conversation with the child about his "betterment"?

These questions, like those of the child, may seem hopelessly large and impossible, ill-fitted to the science we are comfortable with. But perhaps what makes them discomfiting is our long habit of turning away from them and our attempt (always unsuccessful) to escape the meaningful and living language adequate for framing them.

If we could transform our dealings with the child into a genuinely two-way conversation, it might prove healing, not only for the child, but for us adults and our science as well. Then the most important thing might not be our perhaps impertinent question, "How can we make you better?" Rather, it might be how the child's innocent simplicity can counterbalance our sophisticated but one-sided adult constructions. If the child does bring a task to the world, part of it may be to help us become a little more child-like in facing a value-soaked world – fearless in addressing this world with impossibly large questions, and fearless as well in listening for impossibly large answers.

STEVE TALBOTT is editor of the online newsletter, "NetFuture: Technology and Human Responsibility" (NetFuture.org), a publication of The Nature Institute in Ghent, New York (TheNatureInstitute.org). He is a senior researcher at the Institute and is the author of the book, The Future Does Not Compute: Transcending the Machines in Our Midst.

Making Learning to Read a Health-Giving Process

by Arthur M. Pittis

When Rudolf Steiner developed the Waldorf curriculum some ninety years ago, he confronted a paradox that concerned (and still concerns) the teaching of reading. Steiner believed that reading, as an activity dealing with abstractions – printed words that are symbols for things, not things themselves – is for the young child basically an unhealthy activity. Steiner held that the developing child becomes able to deal with abstractions and concepts in a natural and unstressed way only at puberty. Ideally, then, reading should be taught when the child is twelve or thirteen years old.

This idea of course conflicts with the dominant attitude toward reading that existed then as now, namely, that reading is such a critical skill that it should be taught to children at an early age, and the earlier the better. Steiner certainly realized that his new approach to education could not delay the learning of reading until puberty. His challenge was to develop a way of teaching reading that transformed what was otherwise a harmful activity into something nourishing and health-giving for the child. To that end, Steiner designed a unique approach to the teaching of reading. In this approach, the child's development of the ability to read is connected to his own inner development of consciousness as well as to the evolutionary development of human literacy.

The Waldorf kindergarten is essentially a preliterate culture, as far as the child is concerned. No attempt is made to teach children how to read in the traditional academic sense. Even the child's personal cubby usually bears a distinctive, colorful icon, a picture of a bird or chipmunk, perhaps, rather than a name tag.

Also, the kindergarten teacher consciously tries to imbue all the language that the child experiences with beauty. Directions and instructions are usually sung; poems are recited; songs sung; and nature stories and fairy tales told. In all cases of verbal communication, the child experiences elevated language that is different from that which is experienced in the day-to-day language in the home, play, and the media. Central to this way of using language is the pedagogical intention of strengthening the child's ability to form living, inner, imaginative pictures.

This type of early childhood experience works to develop the capacities for language that exist in a non- or preliterate cultural context. Reading, itself, characterizes literate society, but it is not an indispensable or universal human activity. It represents a type of cultural achievement that is not absolutely necessary for human development in the way that keen observation, or manual dexterity, or even facility with arithmetic is. A highly developed, culturally based use of language can exist without reading.

Modern culture obviously values the ability to read and to read at an early age. The communication of information, thoughts, and feelings is largely through the written and printed word. Ours is a culture swimming in print, and the assumption is, then as now, namely, that reading is such a critical skill that it should be taught to children at an early age and that the earlier the better it will be for all. Inevitably, the child absorbs this attitude and learns to place a high value on knowing how to read. Children are as anxious in this regard as parents, grandparents, and most non-Waldorf teachers.

It is against this background that formal reading instruction begins in the Waldorf first grade. The curricular indication by Rudolf Steiner regarding reading is very simple: The child will learn to read through writing, and the activity of writing will arise out of pictorial

representations of the letters. Consonants are pictures of the outer world, and vowels are expressions of the inner state of soul. As in all aspects of Waldorf elementary school education, the learning process should proceed from the whole to the parts and not the other way around. Let consider how this process takes place in first grade.

Imagine that the class teacher creates, in the fairy-tale tradition, a story in which a character is sent on a journey to the sea and must pass over high mountains on the way. While passing through the mountains, the character encounters a snake who guides the journey. Once our seeker arrives at the sea, a fish with magical powers appears atop the waves and provides the knowledge the character has been seeking. In reviewing this story, four key elements – the mountains, the snake, the fish, and the waves – figure prominently. Each of them is something of importance in the outer world that the character must encounter.

The next day, the teacher makes a series of drawings on the board that emphasize these four key elements. The pedagogical intention of these images is to serve as a form of picture-writing out of which specific consonants can be extracted. The mountain becomes the letter M, the snake the S, and the waves of the water the W. These discovered letters become the basis of all sorts of artistically based writing exercises that ultimately focus on the formal skill of handwriting.

Of course, not every consonant letter we use in our modern alphabet is given to this activity, and it would be pedantic to try to fit all our letters into this form. The teacher is free to pick and choose as appropriate; and as for the other consonants, the children can simply be told that they can discover more pictures of their own.

The vowels are of a completely different nature. They are expressions of the inner life of feeling. They reveal the inner gestures of our human soul. In the historical evolution of written language they did not emerge pictographically, as did the consonants. Thus the vowels are not taught in the way described above. Teachers use a variety of approaches. Some draw angelic or human figures making the eurythmy gestures for these sounds. The popular cultural representation, "A is for apple," has no place in the Waldorf classroom. It is aesthetically banal and linguistically false. The long vowel "a" is not even found in the word apple.

What has been described above is simply the introductory lessons in writing/reading that take place in the first half of first grade in most Waldorf classrooms. These lessons comprise a leisurely process, founded on the pedagogical principles that children should not be rushed, that learning must appeal to and be directed through imaginative capacities, and that a subject, even one as seemingly simple as the alphabet, should be explored in a way that guides the children toward an understanding of deeper truths.

Letters by themselves are, of course, a dead end; they need to be combined into words and then the words must be put together to form a sentence. Just as the ancient pictograph was an iconographic representation of a thing in the outer world, the written word, and by extension the written sentence in which it lives, becomes an abstraction of that thing, but an abstraction that is still imbued with the power of imagination and feeling.

Once the process of mastering the form of the letters has begun, the teacher immediately returns to the whole story, its sentences and individual words. New stories are told, and the children begin copying into their main lesson books texts that the teacher has written on the blackboard. This copy work is accompanied by supporting skill work in building sight vocabulary and, to a lesser extent, phonetic decoding. Over time, each of the children, each at his own pace, develops a set of recognizable words – a set that grows day by day – and eventually discovers that he can read.

Let us reflect upon this wonder-filled process and examine how this abstract, intellectual activity is transformed into an ever-expanding and health-engendering one. The key lies in its abstract, intellectual aspect being metamorphosed through a rhythmic alternation of artistically based, purposeful activity and what could be called "soul breathing" (described below).

A story is told by the teacher, and the children take the images evoked into their inner life of feeling and thinking. Next, the story is reviewed through recapitulation and even playacting, and the inner pictures that the children formed are "breathed out" again. The story is now written on the board and, with the teacher's guidance, read aloud and once more inhaled into the inner life of imagination. The children now artistically copy the story into their main lesson books, and it becomes very deeply their own. Imagine the intensity of this activity. And finally, the copied text is once more read aloud, this time from the children's individual pages, and exhaled into the room.

In the early grades, the class teacher will employ this method of instruction, using it to teach the fundamentals of reading. Later, in the middle and upper grades, the method is transformed and used to teach composition, both narrative and expository.

Usually by the middle of the second grade, many children want to read something other than what the teacher has written on the board. They want to test their abilities with "real," printed texts. After all, they are approaching the nine-year change, and the strong, individualized experiences of themselves in the world that this change stimulates are becoming manifest.

At this point, most teachers seek out printed materials for the children to read in school. Ideally this material should consist of engaging and edifying stories that hold the children's interest while supporting the Waldorf school curriculum. On a practical-skills level, these texts need to contain controlled, but increasingly rich, basic vocabulary and increasingly complex types of sentence structure. While the textbook industry has no shortage of these books, what they offer is almost completely devoid of value for the pedagogical intentions of the Waldorf school curriculum. The ongoing cultural war between secular and religious values in our society has seen to this.

To meet this need, I have written a five-volume progressive and remediable Waldorf reader series. The series is published by Waldorf Publications and is available through their online bookstore at www.waldorfpublications.org. I hope that these readers will help children to develop a deep love for reading.

ARTHUR M. PITTIS has been a Waldorf teacher for over twenty-five years, first in Baltimore and currently in Austin, TX. He has led classes through two-and-a-half eight-year cycles and is now teaching high school humanities. He is a member of the AWSNA Leadership Council, representing the Texas-Mexico-Southwest Rockies region. Arthur is the author of Pedagogical Theatre: Dramaturgy and Performance Practice in the Lower and Middle Schools, a very popular resource book for Waldorf class teachers. His two daughters, now young adults, were fortunate enough to have a Waldorf education from kindergarten through high school.

Waldorf and Adolescence

We all vividly remember our high school years. During this span of time, our self-awareness and self-questions were at a pinnacle. Out memories range from despair to elation as we review those exciting but turbulent years. There is no pathway around this stage of life … we must just bear them and proceed straight ahead.

In a Waldorf high school each student is seen as an individual with unique talents needing to be honed and academic skills needing to be rigorously exercised. At the same time the students seek truth in all they encounter, be it the course work or adult interaction. They see the world as theirs and are sheltered by the tempering of hardships and disappointments which age introduces.

The following four articles present the mood of the high school classroom as well as some of the content of the lessons. It is hoped that they will give you more insight as you consider the option of enrolling your son or daughter in a Waldorf high school.

The Magical Mystery Tour of Adolescence

by David Sloan

Astral Storm Coming in: The Ninth Grader

Most high school freshmen have already reached puberty. They find themselves in possession of an inner realm that seems to control them more often than they control it. Parents who have raised a teenager know that the experience is akin to living in an amusement park with the roller coaster constantly whirling around the house. Teenagers at this age are by their very nature extremists, swinging from giddiness to depression, from dreamy unawareness to acute attention within the space of seconds. However, it is important to differentiate between boys and girls at this age, the gap between them is so great that they appear to belong to different species.

For a couple of years at least, it is as if the gods stacked the odds in favor of the girls. As the girls themselves will so readily explain, they are simply more mature than the boys when they enter high school, and, of course, they are right. The girls come into ninth grade ready to dive into and share their burgeoning inner world, while the boys seem somewhat bewildered by all the changes they are undergoing.

Rudolf Steiner explains the huge gender gap at this age in spiritual terms. He points out that, at this age, the incipient forces of the Ego – the forces of our mature and higher Self – permeate the feeling life of girls. Steiner termed our feeling, or soul, life the astral body. This absorption of Ego forces into the feeling realm intensifies girls' awareness of the depth and potency of their emotions. So strongly can girls feel their newfound blend of passion, power, and discernment that, they can become emboldened to the point of sassiness. Steiner suggests that, in contrast, the Ego forces of boys penetrate less into their feelings and more into their physical natures. That may help explain that while the girls become so enamored of and so interested in talking about relationships, in writing feverishly in their secret diaries, and in fantasizing about saving all the homeless children in Calcutta, or perhaps about marrying Johnny Depp, the boys are still out on the playing field punching each other and giving one another wedgies.

Ninth-grade boys can appear to be crude dullards when compared to their female counterparts, by whom they are often dwarfed, sometimes in stature as well as in sheer, overpowering emotional intensity. The girls seem very eager to confront life, while the boys would just as soon hide themselves away until they are better equipped. Jaimen McMillan, founder of Spacial Dynamics – an approach to movement education used in many Waldorf schools – once described this stage of male adolescence by saying that the fourteen-year-old boy might as well wear a sign that says simply "Under Construction" like those building sites that are surrounded by a wall of boards with barbed wire strung around the top.

Fortunately, this gap usually closes by eleventh grade. As one of the feistier boys once remarked to a girl who, for the umpteenth time, had just pointed out how much more mature girls were than boys, "Sure, you girls are more mature for a little while, until the boys pass you by as juniors while you stagnate where you are for the rest of your lives." Despite their differences, both boys and girls at this age live in the polarities of their mood swings.

The Temptations of the World: The Tenth Grader

It is not a hyperbole to say that a dramatic, even radical change takes place between the freshman and sophomore years. Those teachers who deal with adolescents day-to-day and month-to-month will attest to the surprising transformation that can occur in the

summer before the sophomore year. Perhaps it has something to do with having a year of high school already under their belts, or perhaps it can be attributed to natural maturation. In either case, sophomores often return to school in the autumn much fuller of themselves than they were as humbler ninth graders. Instead of seeing them as neophytes flailing about in the aforementioned ninth-grade swamp, we might picture them as the self-assured crew members of a sleek, Greek sailing ship, leaving the protective home harbor, setting out for open water. They  seem more comfortable with themselves and more confident than ever of their cognitive abilities.

Yet we teachers have noticed another pattern that often emerges during tenth grade. Perhaps it can be traced to this newfound confidence that can border on brazenness. Whatever the reason, many sophomores go "overboard" sometime during the year. They get themselves in some kind of trouble – with drugs, sex, stealing, lying. In other words, many tenth graders succumb at one point or another during the year to those myriad temptations the world has to offer.

Is this true for all sophomores? Of course not. Some boys and girls "fall" in sixth or seventh grade, some not until much later. But the general tendency is for this to happen, if it happens at all, sometime in the student's sophomore year.

The Dark Night of the Soul: The Eleventh Grader

What happens to eleventh graders? Why do so many of these ex-sophomores, who were so full of themselves, who just a few months before had exhibited a kind of bluster and swagger and smugness, now in eleventh grade find themselves stricken by a malaise that can be termed a "dark night of the soul"?

Some time ago, a mother of one of my eleventh grade students met with me and shared her concern that her formerly happy-go-lucky, genial, mountain biking son had become evasive, burdened, noncommunicative, and reclusive – almost a stranger to his own mother. This was a single mother describing her only son; she was naturally worried that these changes might indicate some deep psychological problem. Was some heretofore hidden hurt from a childhood trauma bubbling to the surface? Was he using drugs? Had something happened at school between him and his classmates?

So I took this student (whom I shall call Matthew) aside and spent lunch period one day talking to him about his experience of being a junior. He is a wonderful fellow who always appears to have just woken up; in fact, he always looks as if he's just slept in his clothes. But underneath that rumpled exterior is a very astute and articulate young man. Yet when I asked Matthew to describe what he'd been feeling during the fall, he was initially at a loss for words. Is it so surprising that young people can't always express what they're experiencing at the moment! How can we expect them to have much perspective about the very air they breathe, the state of soul that envelops them! As the saying goes, "We don't know who discovered water, but we're pretty sure it wasn't a fish!"

Nevertheless, Matthew was able to describe his recent despondency as "a kind of funk." "I've been in a haze," he said. Then he said something as true of the eleventh-grade experience as any I've heard. He said simply, "I've gone inside." Matthew went on to say that he didn't know if it was a good or bad thing, but that he found himself wandering inwardly. Matthew had begun to discover that he had more inner chambers than he had ever realized before and he was becoming more and more interested in what makes himself tick.

Douglas Gerwin, widely known Waldorf lecturer and a longtime colleague, once characterized this inner exploration in the following manner. Picture a young person, sixteen or seventeen years old, wandering through a large house. She strolls through familiar rooms, looks out to vistas she has known since childhood. Then she notices and opens a door to a wing of the house she never knew existed. She walks down a dark and unfamiliar corridor, her breathing quickening. Without warning, the floorboards beneath her give way. She falls and lands painfully in an even darker, dungeon-like basement, surrounded by eerie shadows and strange, chilling noises. This is akin to the inner "soulscape" experienced by so many juniors – a sudden descent into dark, even forbidding chambers that nevertheless beckon to young people, no matter how awful the potential revelations might be.

During this dark night of the soul, it seems clear that eleventh graders suffer. One of the ways this manifests is as a deeply felt crisis of confidence. Early one fall, I had a tearful meeting with a girl in the junior class – she was the one crying – about how hard everything in her life had become. She was certain that she was the only one in the class who took six hours to do her homework and that, for all her efforts, she was the only one rewarded with mediocre marks. However, I had had nearly the exact same conversation with two of her classmates the week previous! I put these girls in touch with one another so that discovering fellow sufferers might provide some consolation. Yet I really tried to resist the impulse to somehow make these students' struggles less difficult and less painful. Cruel as this sounds, all the angst in the eleventh grade may be both inevitable and, in a certain way, even desirable.

At the Grand Threshold: The Twelfth Grader

I once hosted an evening attended by parents and middle school students. They had come to hear approximately thirty twelfth graders from four different Waldorf high schools speak about their school experiences. The seniors began by recounting their recent, weeklong camping trip to Hermit Island, Maine, where they had studied marine biology, wading in the tide pools of the rocky coast. The students did not simply gather specimens; they examined them under microscopes, sketched the creatures and their environments, wrote poems inspired by Rachel Carson's nature writing, painted seascapes, danced, and sang together.

As the twelfth graders described their activities, a number of them expressed appreciation for the opportunities for hands-on learning. One girl summed up the experience as a reminder that all of nature seems to be quietly urging, "Pay attention" – not only to the spectacular sunsets, but to the understated moments that might otherwise go unnoticed: the skittering of a sand crab across a tide pool floor, the swaying of rockweed in the water, the curving flight of gulls.

Toward the end of the evening, one parent in the audience commented on the students' eloquence, poise, and insight. Indeed, these young people exuded an unpretentious self-assurance that is characteristic of many Waldorf twelfth graders. As contracted and broody as eleventh graders can get, seniors often seem to acquire a new dimension, an expanded awareness that wasn't there before. They stand poised on a great threshold, straddling both the world of the school that they are rapidly outgrowing and the larger world they can't wait to take by storm. Their vision seems to broaden as their thinking deepens. These suddenly larger souls grapple daily with profound questions about their life in the world, the challenge, for example, of how both to express their ever-strengthening individuality on the one hand and at the same time to live in community. And they have a passionate yearning for a new brotherhood of humanity that transcends ethnic and national boundaries.

DAVID SLOAN was born and raised in Southern California. He graduated from Harvard College, received a Waldorf teacher training at Emerson College in England, and is currently completing an MFA in Poetry through the Stonecoast Creative Writing Program at the University of Southern Maine. After more than a quarter century of teaching at the Green Meadow Waldorf School in Chestnut Ridge, NY, David and his wife, Christine, relocated to Brunswick, ME, where he helped to launch a high school for the Merriconeag Waldorf School in Freeport. David's book, Life Lessons: Reaching Teenagers through Literature, *from which the above excerpts are taken, is available from Waldorf Publications at www.waldorfpublications.org.*

What Will Today's Children Need for Financial Success in Tomorrow's Economy?

by Judy Lubin

The growing "creative age" economy calls for the development of human capacities, capacities that Waldorf schools have cultivated for nearly a century.

A Changing Economy

Today's economy is changing. While Waldorf school educators have long believed in the importance of educating children to develop into capable, competent human beings, we are entering a time in which economic success increasingly depends on these same principles. The skills and capacities needed for financial success in the new economy are those that are already a focus of development in Waldorf education: creativity, social skills, self-knowledge, and an inner sense of responsibility or virtue.

A quick look at anecdotal evidence shows a shift in skill categories and job types. Computer programming, work that we used to consider white-collar and highly skilled, is increasingly done, not just outside the United States, but specifically in economies that we would call

developing or less developed. Summarizing various sources, journalist Daniel Pink finds that, within the next two years, one in ten computer or Internet technology (IT) jobs will move overseas. By 2010, one in four will leave the United States. Forrester Research predicts that, by 2015, more than 3 million white-collar jobs, with an accompanying $136 billion in wages, will move to lower-cost countries. Developed nations like Japan and those in Western Europe will see similar patterns of white-collar job movement.

The IT industry is not the only one experiencing this trend. The white-collar financial services industry, over the next five years, will transfer approximately half a million jobs to lower wage areas of the world, according to an AT Kearney estimate.

In almost all cases, the types of white-collar jobs that are leaving economies like ours are those that rely on routine cognitive skills. For example, while computer programming requires cognitive abilities, much programming is routine enough that it can be done by computers themselves, precisely because it is so heavily rule-dependent. The common website development tool InDesign® is just one example of a program that writes programs as it translates graphic displays into HTML code.

Two separate studies, one by NYU economics professor Edward Wolff and the other by Frank Levy and Richard Murnane, economics professors at MIT and Harvard, respectively, have shown that, over the past decades, we have seen little to no growth in jobs that require either manual or routine cognitive skills. The output of routine cognitive, or rule-based, skills is invariably a product that is itself routinely enough produced that it can be coded and sent through a wire. This means that routine cognitive work, like manufacturing, can be done wherever it is cheapest, by a machine or in a low wage country. In Bangalore, India, for example, IT workers currently earn about one-seventh of the wages that the same work used to earn in the U.S. Accordingly, Bangalore is currently absorbing a large portion of outsourced IT work.

In this context, the SATs and other standardized tests, like writing computer programs, require cognitive work, but, precisely because the answers must fit into one of several boxes, can test only routine cognition. Increasingly, those with high SAT scores and little else to

show on college applica-
tions will find themselves
prepared for only low
wage jobs.

The Creative Age

The type of work
that is on the rise and
still earns a decent living
is work that involves not
only uniquely human
skills, as opposed to skills
that a computer can copy,
but skills that are not

standardized across humans. Both Wolff and Levy and Murnane find
that nearly all job growth over the past several decades has come
in the form of jobs requiring complex communication and complex
cognitive work or expert thinking. By "expert thinking," the authors
primarily mean solving problems that have not yet been solved. To
simplify their terminology, job growth has occurred in those jobs that
require creativity and relationships.

Case studies of Silicon Valley show that the manufacture of
commodity products long ago moved offshore. Companies that
remain are those that innovate and those that produce custom
products for a small set of clients. The success of these custom shops
depends substantially on the ability of the people within the company
to maintain stable relationships with clients.

Even if we haven't yet agreed upon a new name – the "creative
age" gets my vote – we have realized that the term "information
age" barely begins to grasp the concept of our current reality. Today,
more Americans are employed in the arts, entertainment, and design
industries than are employed as lawyers, accountants, and auditors.
Compared to the mid 1990s, ten times more people work as graphic
designers. Our economy also has more artists and writers than ever
before.

Using a stringent definition of creative industries that includes
primarily artistic work or innovation, business consultant John Howkins

estimates that the value of the creative economy in 1997 was $2.2 trillion (seven percent of world GDP), and is growing at five percent per year. The United States and other developed countries contain the greatest share of this creative economy.

Attempting to account for changes in the way work itself is done, Carnegie Mellon economics professor Richard Florida uses a more liberal definition of creative work. He finds that more than thirty percent of the work force belongs to the "creative class," a group of people whose primary occupation involves creativity-based human capital and whose numbers now surpass those of the working class. Florida's definition of "creative worker" stretches the common sense definition to include managers and others who perform jobs that still can be done in the old fashioned, noncreative way. This comes from the attempt, however, to recognize that even old jobs are being done differently. UCLA education professor Mike Rose agrees with a multi-industry analysis that finds that, these days, even jobs that we would consider blue-collar require high levels of cognitive capacity.

Their insights are supported by researchers like David Angel, who finds that production engineers in Silicon Valley are responsible for almost as much innovation, through problem solving during manufacturing, as design engineers. Concurrently, these engineers earn substantially higher wages than production engineers in the same

industry, who work under different policies that confine creativity to the design stage. Incidentally, Silicon Valley firms have continually outperformed firms with more hierarchical structures, structures that confine innovation.

Structures

When skimming across the surface of today's new economy, we may wonder if these changes are not just the latest fad. But an examination of these changes at the structural level of the economy shows that we are moving into a time in which broader human skills form the basis for success.

Before examining the structural foundation of the new creative economy more deeply, however, we will explore the structure of the industrial age economy that we are leaving behind. The goal is to trace the economic forces that pressured society to emphasize the human-as-automaton paradigm and to show how the creative economy is reversing this pressure, so that economic success is becoming more aligned with personal goals and the process of becoming human.

The industrial age was a time in which first manual and then routine cognitive skills were emphasized. We have found that the work of both of these skill categories can be replicated by machines. Yet, there is something deeper, at the structural level of the industrial age economy, that reinforced a less human-centered path.

While the industrial age was driven by the creative innovation that led to the machines that then dominated the economy, the machines themselves quickly became more salient than their invention. At the beginning of the industrial age, most of the new machinery was used to increase productivity at pre-industrial tasks, like farming. But, for individual economic success, the important point was not so much the increase in productivity, but, rather, that the machines themselves were scarce. While we had invented our way into higher productivity in many tasks, we had not yet invented a way to produce the machines themselves quickly and easily. Because of its scarcity, machinery generated economic value. Physical capital, not human skill, became the main wealth-creating asset of the economy. Unlike human skill, physical capital is stored externally to humans and is fully transferable from one person to another.

In the industrial age, physical capital did transfer straight up the capitalist hierarchy, despite the clear violation of decentralized economic power required of foundational free market theories. By the early 2000s, the wealthiest 10% held 90% of the nation's marketable wealth. With 40% of the nation's wealth owned by just one percent of the population, our modern democracy is exactly as topheavy as England's monarchy in the 1700s.

In other words, the industrial age was a time in which the single most important capacity for the generation of wealth was wealth itself. This recognition tells us what concerned industrial-age parents wanted to do to ensure their children's success – build wealth and pass it on.

For most, this was easier said than done. With an uneven distribution of capital and an uneven ability to generate new wealth, the industrial age saw a new game that looked surprisingly like the old game of aristocracy. Asset owners needed workers to use the owner's assets for production in the same way that kings needed peasants to work their large land holdings. For asset owners, the ability to be creative and to take risks with their assets led to success. For those who did not own financial assets, success depended on an ability to continue working with someone else's financial assets. The ability to obey became the single most important capacity for financial success for those who had jobs and did not own the means to their livelihood. Our system of public corporations, by the way, ensures that even CEOs have bosses – the shareholders.

Everyone an Entrepreneur

These are some of the very issues that Rudolf Steiner's threefold social organism was meant to address. They are also the very issues that are becoming outdated in the modern economy. To this end, it is useful to remember that Steiner explicitly envisaged his threefold social organism to create a situation in which everyone is an entrepreneur. No person will sell his or her labor, only the product of the labor. There will be no worker-boss relationship as we know it today. Instead, every individual will be in charge of his or her own career. A system of rights will help entrepreneurs negotiate on equal footing, so that economic cooperation can occur in an environment of dignity for everyone.

While this description is a far cry from the industrial-age economy that dominated Steiner's day, it is the very direction in which we are moving. No evidence suggests that we are on track soon to reach the full promise of a threefold social organism. We do, however, increasingly see the need for the same entrepreneurial skills that are needed to make Steiner's vision a reality. Further, the primary assets that creative economy participants use to ply their entrepreneurial talents are those that are uniquely human in nature. In other words, educating the whole human being is becoming an economic necessity, not simply an alternative lifestyle choice.

We must expect that we will invent ourselves into a new system that is more in keeping with the entrepreneurial nature of a human-based economy. The uneven wealth distribution brought about during the industrial age means that the "have-nots" have the same incentives to overthrow the "haves" as peasants had to overthrow an unjust monarchy. Rather than revolution, however, incentives also exist to invent a new system around the old, as we are currently doing.

We do not live in a world in which everyone is an entrepreneur, but we are much closer now than we were during the industrial age. Pink estimates that, in 2001, thirty percent of Americans were entrepreneurs, in that they were self-employed, contract workers, or involved in a micro-business of fewer than four employees. Although large corporations, because of their political power, still predominate, the number of smaller companies is on the rise. Today, more than half of U.S. businesses, and ninety percent of engineering firms, are micro-businesses.

With high rates of job turnover in modern times, even many of those who work for large companies do so with an understanding that the employment relationship is but a part of the career that they themselves manage. By the mid-1990s, economist Henry Farber found that, for the entire economy, approximately half of all jobs last less than one year. In creative economies like Silicon Valley, these numbers can be even higher. Up to sixty percent of Silicon Valley engineers quit in a given year, with almost eighty percent of resignations reflecting movement to another Silicon Valley job, showing that, instead of being committed to a single firm in the fashion of the late industrial age, these engineers are committed to their own careers in the

Valley. Management expert Suzy Wetlaufer interviewed some of these highly successful high-tech workers and found that they will stay at a company only if the work delivers a constant stream of growth and challenge that engages their hearts and minds.

Not only is the creative economy more entrepreneurial, but its roots are structured differently. By the 1980s, economic and sociological researchers had coined the term "agglomeration economy" for areas like Silicon Valley that were the beginnings of what Howkins and others now call the creative economy. These agglomeration economies both begin with and thrive on an influx of human thinking capacities. While the ability to continually increase aggregate levels of human cognition is the make-or-break criterion, a snowball effect means that the more competent workers an area has, the easier it is to attract even more workers, each of whom values working with other competent people. Growth becomes endogenous and the area experiences high levels of innovation and high levels of new start-ups.

Florida goes further to find that the whole of today's economy is moving toward an agglomeration style and that success today depends upon the level to which any area can master the three Ts: Technology, Talent, and Tolerance (openness to new ideas, cognitive flexibility).

Technology, of course, encompasses more than just computers and machines. The machines themselves are actually the product of the process of technology, which represents the know-how and ability to create a tangible product. Indeed, since machines like laptop computers are so cheaply and easily available, the cognitive aspects of technology are more readily apparent in the process. Technology, then, is dependent upon human cognitive capacities, as are talent and tolerance. In other words, the human being is the economic driver of the modern economy, a stark contrast to the machine-driven economy of the industrial age.

There is both good news and bad news in this realization. The good news is that an economy in which the main resources reside within individual humans should lead to a wider dispersion of economic resources. We also have an opportunity to experience a more entrepreneurial environment. As owner of his or her own cognitive assets, everyone is an entrepreneur. The bad news comes from the flip side of the same argument. Since we can't directly transfer today's economic assets without teaching and experience, society cannot simply hand economic success to its children. Instead, we must help them to develop their own human capacities. It should be noted that the United States is quickly slipping from its leadership of the creative economy and that its "innovative infrastructure" is decaying.

Creative Capacities

Let's take a closer look at the capacities that workers in today's and tomorrow's creative economy will need to develop in order to succeed. Of course, in a creative economy, they will need the capacity of creativity: the ability to create value from the combination of human ingenuity and raw materials. While parts of the new economy are making use of artistic creativity, the underlying skills are those of creative problem solving and innovation in general. Levy and Murnane see it as the ability to solve a problem that has not yet been solved, which includes the ability to think flexibly about technical problems, social problems, and all manner of other problems. But the capacity of creativity also includes the ability to run the entire creative process from idea generation to, potentially, the formation of a process or tangible product. In this use of the term, thinking, feeling, and willing, qualities well known to Waldorf educators, are all necessary components.

Because they will be plying their own human assets in their entrepreneurial endeavors, today's children will need to know how to make full use of their human assets. In other words, they will need to know themselves. To make money from something as simple as a machine requires an understanding of how the machine works. The same is true of our own human resources when we put those resources to the money-making tasks in our lives. Included in this capacity is the ability to know one's skills and interests, the ability to muster the self-confidence needed to take a creative risk, the ability to get oneself into the high productivity state of "flow," as psychologist Mihaly Csikszentmihalyi calls it, and much more.

We can discover additional necessary capacities by examining the form and structure of modern economies. A typical industrial- or financial-age firm is organized in a hierarchical manner, as is the industry itself. It can be charted as a pyramid, with the CEO on top and layers of increasing numbers below. Firms are connected by

formal ownership, by rigid ownership-like legal agreements, or by competitors.

Agglomeration economies, like Silicon Valley, however, are organized by dynamic, flexible networks of firms and of people. They can be charted as a pattern of interconnected "players" with little or no implied hierarchy. Relationships or "soft" contracts – agreements to work things out when a disagreement arises – replace the formal ownership arrangements and exacting legal contracts used by industrial-age industries. Competition and cooperation are interspersed, with the same companies sometimes facing each other both as competitors and as partners.

In this world, relationships matter. UCBerkeley Information Management Professor AnnaLee Saxenian finds that all business in Silicon Valley flows through a rich network of people and that these relationships determine everything from new firm formation to daily work flow. In the modern economy, as a whole, relationships matter. Princeton economist Alan Blinder and his colleagues find that eighty-five percent of nonfarm goods and services are sold to people with whom the firm has an ongoing relationship. Since a firm is not a person, these relationships must be managed by the people within the firm.

Relationships Matter

The formation of London's St Luke's advertising agency is a case in point. In 1995, Omnicon bought the advertising agency of Chiat/Day. Fearing layoffs, the people of Chiat/Day's London office did not want to be under Omnicon's control. En masse, the employees quit Chiat/Day and started a new company, St Luke's, which maintained all previous client relationships and operated just as it had under the Chiat/Day name, leaving Omnicon holding an empty bag. Omnicon may have owned the "company," but the employees owned the relationships with the clients. The company's entire value was stored in the client relationships.

Relationships matter not just because the economy is structured by levels of relationships among firms, but because the primary economic assets reside within individuals. Before an innovation becomes a marketable product, it is an idea that lives within the mind of the innovator. Few ideas get to market without the help of other ideas. This means that the people holding correlative ideas must work together in order to create tangible products. Relationships and interpersonal cooperation are part and parcel of the creative economy.

The emphasis on relationships brings to light another necessary capacity. In an economy in which relationships and "soft" contracts replace exacting legal obligations, trust and trustworthiness become essential. If Chiat/Day's employees had trusted Omnicon not to implement mass layoffs, they would not have left Omnicon with an expensive empty shell of a company. A reputation for trustworthiness is an important asset in the creative economy. Developing such a reputation requires the ability to act with responsibility and with a sense of ethics. I call this capacity virtue, although many other terms could be used.

Success, then, in the type of economy toward which we are moving and that today's children will experience, depends upon the capacities of creativity, self-knowledge, social skills, and virtue, however labeled. The main point is that today's children will need to succeed on the terms of entrepreneurs and not as laborers. There is evidence to suggest that these skills, or something akin to them, have always been necessary for success. We are, however, coming, in the mainstream, to an increased understanding of their importance.

Downsides

While I have so far painted a fairly rosy picture of the creative economy, we should note that there are downsides to this change. I have worked in the bastions of both industrial capitalism – Wall Street – and the creative economy – Silicon Valley. In every manner, I experienced Silicon Valley as a place more supportive of human beings and of human ideals, as well as a more enjoyable and more egalitarian place to work. Working in the Valley, however, was no walk in the park. Hours were long, high levels of responsibility were expected, and I would not have survived without a continually fueled inner drive.

In general, in the creative economy individual markets and firms are notoriously unstable, even as the system itself remains stable. For those who do not manage personal change well, the level of flexibility required by the creative age may bring about nostalgia for the industrial age. Further, while the cooperative nature of creative age markets does ease competition, this can be a double-edged sword. With a minor decrease in competitiveness, there is more room for everyone to breathe and plenty of room for cooperation. But, if easing competitiveness goes unchecked, we can easily find a single firm dominating an entire market, a situation that rings of exploitation, not of freedom.

Most important, even though there is clearly a push toward a more human-focused economy, the dehumanizing forces that took hold during the industrial age are far from banished. As during any change, a careful eye on the direction of the change and a strong participative hand are needed to ensure that the creative economy lives up to its more humanizing potential.

We can take heart, however, from the understanding that, increasingly, parents will face less pressure to socialize their children to fit into a dehumanizing system and will be increasingly interested in finding an education system that emphasizes fuller human capacities like creativity, cognitive flexibility, social skills, and the will force of an entrepreneur. Waldorf education, with its foundations in the entrepreneurial environment of Steiner's envisaged threefold social organism, has long been prepared for this challenge.

JUDY LUBIN holds a PhD in economic theory from the University of Chicago. Her research focuses on the structure and organization of firms, markets, and employment in a post-industrial economy. She is also an active parent volunteer at the Chicago Waldorf School.

A full edition of this abbreviated paper and all footnotes can be found in Research Bulletin, *Volume 12,#1.*

Shakespeare and the Eleventh Grader:
A Match Made in Heaven

by David Mitchell

As a Waldorf high school teacher, you can observe a distinct change of mood in the students after they have passed from their sophomore to their junior year. This mood change is evident in a more inward, contained, self-aware composure. The transition is subtle but significant. It could also be characterized as a move to a more mature form of thinking. The eleventh grader has acquired the capacity to form an internal space for reflection. In the previous two years in high school, they were vacillating between inner and outer. Now they have the ability both to hold and to create experiences within the confines of their own soul life. The eleventh grader asks many questions about life. Curiously, most of these questions begin with the word "Why?"

William Shakespeare also frequently asked this kind of question. He was able to look behind the gossamer veils of everyday reality and, through drama, to portray intense inner struggles dealing with passion, thinking, death, life, and the entire gamut of human emotions. He can be viewed as the herald of modern self consciousness.

An intense study of Shakespeare for eleventh graders can deepen their self knowledge, help them to understand life, and enrich their souls through the beauty of his art. It allows students, at a time when their self awareness is still fragile, to look at sensitive and perhaps intimidating personal issues through the characters in the plays. Also, a skillful teacher can use Shakespeare to exercise the students' power of analytical thinking. Finally, the study of Shakespeare can help students become more aware of their own humanity. As they explore the influence of sin and virtue in Shakespeare's heroes, observe that happiness is dependent on the control of the passions, and see that knowledge is gained by living a humane, moral, and "mannerly" life, they learn valuable lessons for living. Shakespeare's characters demonstrate that goodness of thought, if constantly cultivated, will become a habit.

There are challenges for the teacher, though. The class may be apathetic at the outset. They will find Shakespeare's language awkward and, on first reading, often hard to understand. The students may be resistant and question the relevance of studying the works of a man who lived four hundred years ago.

Begin the first lesson by arousing interest through a discussion of language. You can ask the class how many words they think they use in their daily vocabulary. Common words such as *people, three, the, funny, run, chair, book*, and *school* are given as examples. There is always a wide range of guesses, and the students are surprised to learn that a well-read person in today's society knows about 6000 words. Then you can point out that this is about 2000 words less than it was at the turn of the century, before electronic media, when people read much more.

Now the students are introduced to the biography of Shakespeare and his time. Shakespeare lived from 1564–1616. At that time, speech and poetry played a different role in people's lives than they do today. Not yet embalmed in dictionaries, language and speech were alive and expressed not only thoughts but also feelings of the heart. And poetry, revered as the language of the angels, was a part of everyday life. Still possessing the warmth of feeling of medieval times, Shakespeare's audience was able to receive poetry in a different way than we do today.

In Shakespeare's day, the period of the "High Renaissance," the English Empire was expanding around the globe. England was emerging as Europe's dominant political force, and English was becoming the "world" language. Shakespeare wrote 36 plays, 154 sonnets, and various longer poems. In his work, he introduced 9000 new words into the English language, more than all the other English poets combined. Shakespeare coined such common words as *critic, disheartened, advantageous, radiant, generous, obscene, pious,* and *dwindle.* He took slang words and moved them into common usage: *fireworks, hubbub, jitterbug, exciting, hectic, bogus, striptease,* and *clumsy.* He put words together into phrases that we use today, such as: a tower of strength, zoot suit, sit down strike, whodunit, milk of human kindness, and boom and bust.

Shakespeare was a verbal genius with a profound sympathy for the human condition. He was a man of keen humor and great sweetness of mind, who turned every sentence he wrote into a melody. Computers estimate that Shakespeare had an active vocabulary of over 25,000 words. He refers to over 100 species of birds and over 150 varieties of plants in his plays. Usually, this introduction awakens the students' interest and convinces them that the study of Shakespeare is something important for them.

The study of Shakespeare includes, of course, the study of the world in which he lived. Life in Elizabethan England was rich and exciting. Explorers were returning from newly discovered lands with exotic beasts and strangely dressed natives. At one time, the Tower of London housed a giraffe, a rhinoceros, and a kangaroo! Street life was a carnival. Walking over London Bridge, you might come across a flame swallower, a bear on a chain going to the bear baitings, a crocodile on a tether, cocks fighting in a rope ring, or gymnasts leaping through the air.

The theater was a place of gay and abundant entertainment where this rich life was concentrated. A theater-goer might spend three hours dressing for the occasion, putting on a powdered wig, a ruff or starched collar, elaborately polished boots or shoes with gold buckles, a farthingale or wide hoop skirt with a wire cage beneath (often weighing thirty pounds or so), plus layers of chiffon and lace. The clothes were of rich colors and heavily embroidered, often with silver or gold thread, and sewn with jewels. Since hats were worn both indoors and out, a hat, perhaps of fantastical shape, would be part of the theater-goer's attire. Courtiers wore their fortunes on their backs and went to the theater to see and to be seen, as well as to watch the play. Living was a spectator sport!

Shakespeare wrote in this milieu. He wrote first to entertain but also to stimulate the mind. Behind his work lay a deep study of humankind and the issues of human life. He understood that to the Elizabethans a thought was not an abstraction; it was an experience.

The eleventh grade Shakespeare block (meeting for ninety minutes a day for about three weeks) begins, as I teach it, with the study of about twenty of the more well known speeches: Hamlet's "To Be or Not To Be," Romeo's "Thus with a Kiss I Die," "Such Stuff as Dreams Are Made of" from *The Tempest*, et al. Most students have encountered these speeches before. We take turns, reading the speeches aloud. We analyze them and become familiar with Shakespeare's modes of expression.

With this background and with the students' interest aroused, we now plunge into one of the plays. There are many levels of Shakespeare's work. There are the comedies, the tragedies, the histories, and the four "resurrection plays" written at the end of his life.

I like to begin with an earthy romance, such as *The Taming of the Shrew*. This play really appeals to adolescents and allows for a deep discussion of interpersonal relationships, a part of life students at this age are struggling to explore and understand. I use The Folger Library's General Shakespeare Reader series. Its side page explanations, pronunciation guides, introductions and critical essays are all excellent.

Parts are assigned, and we read the play out loud, relishing the battles of the sexes that take place and being tickled by the turns of speech. We discuss the intentions of Petruccio and the hardness of Katarina. We listen to tape recordings of accomplished actors and take note of their inflection, their voice modulation, and their rendering of the puns, conceits, asides, and double entendres. The students then take the play home to reread it, to "mine" for words and phrases of importance to be noted and presented to the class the next day.

After reading the play, we start asking "why" questions. Why did Petruccio come to Padua? Why did Kate act so brutishly to her suitors? Why did Bianca's personality change after marriage? Why do we judge people on first meeting? Why must we find some way to bring the polarities of masculine and feminine together so that humanity can evolve?

Aristotle said, "The greatest thing by far is to be master of the metaphor. It is the sign of original genius and implies intuitive perception." We look for metaphors and similes in the play and practice writing our own.

We then read "The Doctrine of the Humours" by Dr. William Harvey, a contemporary of Shakespeare. Harvey's discovery of the circulation of blood was instrumental in changing the practice and theory of medicine. Before Harvey, medicine was based on the belief that there are four bodily "humors" or fluids which determine a person's temperament. Many of Shakespeare's characters have an excess of one humor or another and thus have a clear and particular personality or temperament. Harvey's paper helps the students to understand a belief commonly held in the High Renaissance and to recognize "types" of personalities.

I then choose a play according to the nature and needs of the class. Among the plays we commonly work with are: *The Merchant of Venice, Hamlet, Othello, Macbeth, Romeo and Juliet, The Tempest*, and *The Winter's Tale*. The play chosen is carefully worked through. We act it out. We analyze it. We "mine" it for striking words, phrases, and speeches. Each play provides a theme for an essay.

We look at the structure of the play and at poetic meter. We start with iambic pentameter. Ten students are called to the front to represent the ten syllables in a line. The first person bends over and acts weak, the next stands straight and strong, and so on down the line, weak and strong alternating. A line is read by the group, with the strong "performing" the accent. Next, they are paired up in the buddy system, and we discover we have five iambic feet. When the strong syllable precedes the weak, we have a trochee. The important thing is to let the students act it out, to let them experience it in action. Then they will remember it with their entire being.

Finally, the last day of the block approaches. We have had many different experiences with the material. We have played characters and become intimate with them. We have discussed Shakespeare's idea of sin and of virtue and his comparison of death and sleep. We have constantly asked the question, "Who is (Wo)Man?" We have touched on the many aspects of Shakespeare's genius – his understanding of people, his skill with words, his sense of drama, and his ability to please his audience.

Now I ask the class to suggest a word that expresses the deepest level of human connection. The word "love" is frequently suggested. I ask the students to describe what they love, and I write down their replies on the blackboard. The list may read: "I love my girlfriend (or boyfriend), my mom, my dog, peanut butter and jelly sandwiches, walking barefoot on the beach, having my back scratched," and so forth.

Immediately we begin to see the problem. In English, the word "love" has many different connotations. Because the junior year is one in which we often have exchanges from Waldorf schools in other parts of the world, I might ask the Norwegian student how they say "love." The word is *elsker*. "I love you" is *Jeg elsker deg*. The word relates only to a human being. You cannot elsker a peanut butter and jelly sandwich! We also look at the German word *Liebe*, the French *amour*, and the Spanish *amor*. Each has its own uniqueness and possesses a certain vagueness.

Then we reflect that our study was the "rebirth" of the great cultures of classical Greece and Rome. We find that the Greeks have four words for love: *agape, philios, eros,* and *storgé. Agape* refers to spiritual love, one's love for humanity (a totally outward, giving to others type of love); *philios* is brotherly love, the love of a friend or colleague of either sex; *eros* is erotic or passionate love between two people (a totally inward, taking for oneself type of love); *storgé* is the love of a parent for a child or a child for a teacher.

Every eleventh grader is willing to discuss "love" in its various forms. We discuss these realities for a time as they exist in our own lives. Then we return to Shakespeare and analyze King Lear's relationship with Cordelia, Desdemona's with Othello, Romeo's with Juliet, Petruccio's with Kate, et al. We see that we understand the nature of the human being only when we understand love. And we can only truly love when we understand. And to understand, one must use one's thinking.

In this way, we are able to go below the surface of Shakespeare's works; each student is able to sound the depths of his soul. We wrestle with feelings and thoughts and questions about life that are as real as when Shakespeare depicted them in drama over four hundred years ago.

During Elizabethan times, the human being was thought to be a battleground where an ever changing, constant battle between good and evil is being fought. The deeds and sufferings of the soul are a path of development. The Renaissance man felt that we come to earth in order to meet difficulties that we cannot meet in Heaven. We overcome these difficulties, not by escaping or avoiding them, but by confronting and penetrating them. This is how we grow. Shakespeare wasn't simply concerned with plots; he was interested in how human souls interact and how they metamorphose.

The poet Robert Browning said, "When the fight begins within a man, then he's worth something." And Rudolf Steiner said, "If more people would take up the inner battle, then outer battles would be less likely to occur." By now, the students realize that behind Shakespeare's drama is a profound understanding of life and that each of us needs, in his own way, to engage in the inner struggle for personal development.

There was more than human personality working in Shakespeare. There was the spirit of the whole of human evolution working within him. When the eleventh grader encounters the study of Shakespeare at the correct time in his development, there can be a profound effect: an appreciation of literature and philosophy; a sense of the complexity of the human psyche; a beginning understanding of one's self; and a capacity to analyze oneself, human life, and the world – all these can emerge. Tools of comprehension can be developed and inner pictures built up that will provide strength throughout life. Such are the goals of Waldorf education.

DAVID MITCHELL was Chairman of Publications for the Association of Waldorf Schools of North America (AWSNA) and Co-Director of the Research Institute for Waldorf Education. A past member of the U.S. Department of Education's Private School Leadership Committee, he was a Waldorf teacher for 40 years—as a class teacher for grades 1–8 and as a high school teacher of life sciences, literature, woodwork, blacksmithing, and copper chasing. He was an adjunct professor in education at Antioch University. The Amgen Corporation honored him by selecting him as one of the top two teachers (K–12) in Colorado in 1997.

What Is Phenomenology?

by Michael D'Aleo

Introduction

I recall standing in the checkout line of a large store a few years ago. There were still a couple of people in front of me who were paying for their purchases when a woman came up behind me with her approximately three-year-old child. The woman first glanced at the long line and then noticed a simple child's puzzle near the checkout. The simple puzzle had three or four wooden cutouts that fit nicely into the flat piece of wood from which they had been cut. Each piece was cut in the shape of a barnyard animal and was painted appropriately. "Look," the woman said to the child, "This is a sheep!" With this exclamation she removed a particular piece of wood that was shaped and painted in the outline of a sheep.

Immediately, I saw a problem. "That's not a sheep," I thought to myself. "That's only a cutout piece of wood painted to represent a sheep. A sheep is much larger, has a particular smell, makes a very characteristic sound, its body is covered with a very unusual material that feels soft, often oily and leaves a funny scent and taste on your hand. Have you ever helped someone try and catch some sheep or helped to shear them? Sheep are fast, skittish, they can jump. …These animals have many unusual ways of behaving. …This is only a part of my experience of sheep. Please, take the child somewhere where he can have an experience of sheep!"

I never said anything to the woman or her child, but this moment makes clear what the distinction between a concept that is given and one that arises out of actual sense experiences.

Having a young child of my own, I sympathized with the plight of the woman and her child. The checkout lines in many stores are often designed to overwhelm you as each item competes for your attention and interest. As an adult, we can develop the capacities to ignore or "tune out" the myriad impressions that bombard us in such an environment; a child cannot. However, without careful discrimination we as adults can just as easily begin to "tune out" the many other sense impressions in our world. When this happens, we can begin to sense that our life has become a routine in which we are simply going through the motions, that we have lost our connection to not only the world but also ourselves.

A Brief Historical Context

Many teachers, parents and perhaps older students may have heard that Waldorf education encourages the use of a phenomenological approach to science. While even saying the word "phenomenological" can be difficult for a person encountering it for the first time, there is even less familiarity with the meaning of the word and its relation to the approach to science advocated by many Waldorf schools. In fact, phenomenology does not have its origin in Waldorf education, but instead, the roots of phenomenology can be traced back to European continental philosophy of the late 17th and early 18th centuries. While many people familiar with Waldorf schools may know that Goethe (1749–1832) and Steiner (1861–1925) advocated such an approach, there were parallel efforts by Alexander Gottlieb Baumgarten (1714–1762), Johannes Müller (1801–1858) and Edmund Husserl (1859–1938).

Additionally, in reading any of the writings of the great historical scientists, one finds repeated references to a process that can be described as seeing a "pattern or lawfulness" in observations that had not been seen before or had been simply overlooked by others. Examples of this can be found in the notebooks of Leonardo da Vinci, the dialogues of Galileo Galilei, and the notebooks of Johannes Kepler. In each of these cases, a deeper understanding of a given set of phenomena is reached not by accepting the work of their predecessors, but instead, by looking again at the phenomena described by others and then "seeing something new."

For example, in Galileo's time (early 1600s) the commonly accepted view of objects that fall "naturally" (simply dropped) was that a heavier object would fall faster than a lighter one. By carefully reviewing the argument that was made to support this view, Galileo noticed an inconsistency in the argument. Through a combination of intuitions, experiments, and actual demonstrations, he was able to conclude that all "heavy" objects (ignoring feathers, dust, etc.) would fall through the same distance in the same amount of time, that each object's speed (velocity) would increase at the same rate and, furthermore, that the rate of acceleration was constant. This example is often used in the 10th grade Waldorf Physics block in the study of mechanics.

Another clear example advocating for an experiential approach can be found in da Vinci's notebook in which he describes the difficulties he had with the scholars of his day. In da Vinci's time (about 1500), much of the scholarly debate in universities focused on how to interpret the work left by the "Masters" rather than an individual inquiry into the phenomena of the world. This of course was at odds with da Vinci's own process of keen observation. In *The Notebooks of Leonardo da Vinci* as translated by Edward McCurdy (Reynal & Hitchcock, New York, 1938), the first entry reads:

> If indeed I have no power to quote from authors as they
> (i.e., the scholars) have, it is a far bigger and more worthy
> thing to read by the light of experience, which is the
> instructress of their masters. They strut about puffed up
> and pompous, decked out and adorned not with their own
> labors but by those of others, and they will not even allow
> me my own. And if they despise me who am an inventor,
> how much more should blame be given to themselves, who
> are not inventors but trumpeters and reciters of the work
> of others.

Consciously observing the phenomena of the world: This is the starting point for the middle school science curriculum.

The Approach

A phenomenological approach to science begins with the premise that all empirical knowledge must start with sensory impressions. Every concept we form, be it in science or everyday life, must be based ultimately upon sense impressions or a combination of sense impressions and other concepts. Initially we can think of these sense impressions as the basic senses we use every day such as sight, sound, taste, touch and smell. In time we may become conscious of other sense impressions, for example our senses of motion, balance, thoughts, and so forth.

The foundations for such an approach to an understanding of the world were outlined in depth by Rudolf Steiner, the founder of Waldorf educational methods, in his book *The Philosophy of Freedom* or *Intuitive Thinking as a Spiritual Path*. One of the central themes in this book might be outlined in the following manner.

When we experience a new or unfamiliar environment for the first time, we choose specific observations to focus on and then mentally remove these details from the whole of the environment in which we are observing. There are myriad choices of possible observations, but we can focus on only a finite number at any time. Having decided to focus on specific observations, we then find relationships or order within these observations. Relationships also appear between the observations that have been separated and the whole environment from which they were removed. Initially, one can think of the observations as sense-based perceptions and the relationships as thought-based conceptions. Later on, when the capacity to distinguish between perceptions and conceptions is more clearly developed, one can also take thought as the basis of perceptions as well.

The fascinating part of the process outlined above is that the activity of looking for the relationships between the perceptions is not a linear one nor one that can be arrived at through logic. The process of finding the relationship for the "first time" is often referred to as intuition. Intuition is the process by which one first has an insight into a conceptual framework that can unite a given set of perceptions or a set of perceptions with other concepts. This is the "aha" or "eureka" experience of the scientist, inventor, artist or investigator.

In that moment a new relationship is seen, and it is then and only then that logic can be rightly applied to determine if the relationship will hold true in the context of the other relationships that are known. This process of looking for a relationship among phenomena is the true activity of thinking. Thinking is not simply the recollection of previously known facts.

And herein lies the biggest distinction between a phenomenological educational approach to science and a more conventional educational approach. In a phenomenological approach, one strives to give the students an experience of the phenomena and then have them wrestle with finding relationships or order. This process actually cultivates the true powers and capacities necessary for thinking. Here thinking becomes an activity, a verb, something that is dynamic and living.

In a more conventional approach, the laws or relationships are given initially and then the student is guided through a proof of why they hold true. In this second approach, the students do not need to utilize their own thinking capacities since they simply need to follow a logical argument rather than have an insight themselves as required in the phenomenological approach. In this second case, the thinking becomes a process of data acquisition and accessing.

What is interesting about these two approaches is that in fact almost every new idea and invention that has arisen in science has resulted from a person consciously or unconsciously using a phenomenological approach. Often this can result unconsciously when a scientist is working with an old concept, one that has often been passed down for years, and suddenly the scientist sees something new in the phenomena. In that moment, the scientist leaves the conventional view of looking at the problem using old fixed concepts and instead, becomes interested in some new detail and suddenly desires to "make sense" of this new situation.

This is precisely the kind of thinking that we are ultimately trying to instill in the students in a Waldorf school. It does not necessarily matter whether they are going to become scientists. The sciences give us an opportunity to develop in every student the capacity to enter a situation, take stock of it (make observations) and then make sense of the situation (find relationships and form concepts).

The Young Child

Now of course one cannot initially ask that a young child participate in such a process. To make observations, one needs to have senses that are well developed and have a rich background of experience with which to make comparisons. What is more, a young child needs to experience for herself how to separate out specific sense impressions from the rich world of experiences that are possible to be perceived.

And finally, the world or sensory environment that a child does experience needs to be one in which none of the impressions is either overwhelming or too narrow in its context. To properly educate the very young child, it is not so much a question of "teaching," but rather one of ensuring that the proper environment, one that is rich in sensations and also deep in context, can occur.

Perhaps no environment can surpass nature in its richness of sensations or depth of context. Again, the key is not to teach the child to see the observations and then tell them the concept, but rather to allow this process to occur naturally while the senses of the child are developing.

Recall the example given at the beginning of this essay concerning a sheep. Take a few moments to focus on the environment and sense impressions found on a small farm. Now, compare those to the impressions found in a checkout line at a large store or, to focus on the sheep more specifically, consider the impressions given by an interactive computer program in which animated images of sheep move across a flat screen accompanied with corresponding digitized sounds. Which of these environments will a young child be able to "take in" and which gives the child a richer, fuller context in which to know not only an individual sheep, but the full context of forces and activities that help define how sheep "are"?

It might now be even more apparent why the classrooms for the Waldorf kindergarten students are organized in the way they are and why the activities of the morning circle and "play" are such a central part of a child's "education."

The Middle School Years

Skipping ahead now to the middle school students, we can see that they are definitely in a different place with respect to their individual relationships to the environment and their own self-awareness. By sixth grade the students become very observant of their surroundings. They begin to really notice all of the "odd things" about the adults in their lives and also can become self-conscious of his, or her, own outer appearance and inner feelings.

It is at this time that a teacher can start working consciously with the students' own observations, both those of the individual as well as those shared collectively by the class. The students can be shown a scene such as a sunrise and then later, the teacher can ask them to recall specific observations that were made, what the order was in which they occurred and if there are any relationships (concepts) that can be found between the observations (perceptions).

For example, in the 6th grade I took the class into a small, completely dark, room and, using a high quality light dimmer, ever so slowly increased the level of illumination in the room from total darkness to incredible brilliance (we used a 500 watt bulb). This exercise was done with little talking but I was careful to increase the level of illumination in stages so that the students could really "take in" the phenomena.

During the review period the next day, the students were overflowing with observations. It started with the obvious such as, "At first, I couldn't see anything and then I saw someone's head!" After trying to figure out whose head it was, another student offered, "Initially everything was in black and white," while another said, "and it was also kind of 'flat,' two-dimensional like."

As I slowly focused the conversation, the class began to order their perceptions and noticed that the "scene" started with little to see other than the very dim glow of the lamp. Slowly varying shades of darkness were perceived, and out of this the students began to distinguish familiar forms (a classmate's head). The students then began to notice that some colors on their clothing were more easily discernible during the "darker phases" than other colors. White was seen early on, but it took a brighter level of illumination to distinguish white from yellow. Red was also seen fairly early on, while a relatively bright level of illumination was needed to identify a blue stripe on a sweater that had a black appearance under lower levels of illumination. By the time the light bulb was at its maximum level of brightness, we were all "blind" again, as all we could see was white brilliance. One of the key points the students finally articulated was that the colors changed with the level of illumination. Less obvious but equally present was the role that color plays in our ability to take a two-dimensional image of color and form, and relate it to our everyday three-dimensional spatial orientation. This was just touched upon, as it would become clearer through their experiences in painting class and their study of Renaissance art in 7th grade.

The middle school years is also the time that the students can first make a basic distinction between the world as observed and the world as conceived. The students of this age are not ready for a philosophical exploration of the foundations of knowledge, but it is appropriate to make a distinction between what one actually sees (smells, hears, and so forth) and the feelings and thoughts that arise from these sensations. Again, the teacher does not have to go into a deep philosophical discussion with the students but instead can simply point out the distinction within the context of comments made by students in the class.

The pedagogical importance of helping a young adolescent see the difference between sensations and feelings or thoughts is probably apparent. Here the science lesson presents an opportunity to properly balance the strong feeling life of the early teenager, without resorting to any moralizing.

It is important to be clear about how one might deliver a lesson using a phenomenological approach. First, with little to no introduction, the class is brought into an environment in which the phenomena that are to be discussed the following day are observed. There need be no elaborate scientific setup and, in fact, by bringing the lesson out of regularly encountered environments, the students can develop a sense for how the phenomena in question relate to the world at large.

As the activity or process unfolds, the students should be encouraged to observe the phenomena as fully as possible with minimal prodding from the teacher to "look at this" or "did you hear that?" At the same time, the students should be discouraged from communicating in any manner or asking questions out loud. Finally, when the experience or experiment has been completed, and just before the class finishes, the students can be asked to recall or remember the sequence of events. The importance of having the students live with the process (sequencing is an important tool for clear thinking) they have just observed should not be overlooked. Sometimes a teacher can leave the students with a question to consider, but the teacher should always be careful not to lead the students toward a conclusion.

On the following morning, the teacher has the students recall the demonstration from the previous day but without redoing the experiment or using the apparatus as a prop. The teacher's first request of the students should be to solicit observations without conclusions, cause or relationships. This process allows each of the students to carefully weigh and consider all of the observations without having a sense that they have to rush ahead and get "the answer" before their classmates.

Additionally, the teacher needs to be careful not to have too strong a picture of what the students, "should have observed" and what the exact wording is of "what they should conclude." If one has cultivated the right atmosphere in the class, the students will arrive at not only the observations and conclusions that were anticipated, but also will often bring other observations and find additional relationships that were not intended. Again, the teacher needs to be very awake to allow for the possibility of new ways of seeing a relationship and other means of expressing a given relationship.

We want the students to experience that they are truly involved in forming the concepts and not simply trying to say "what the teacher wants me to say." Again, the relationships or concepts are only developed after all of the observations are in place. It is also important that the teacher not immediately judge a comment as "correct" or "incorrect" but, instead, allow the class to try to form the judgment of whether or not a suggested relationship offered by one of the students holds true.

In the end, the teacher must be the guide of the class, but the process does not always have to move forward because the teacher is always the first to take "the next step." In fact, the best opportunity to introduce the next demonstration or experience can often arise when a student who has just understood the previous day's material, asks a question such as, "Well if that's true, then what about...?" When this happens, it is usually a sign that things are going well.

An Example

I can recall how many of these elements came together for the first time during a specific lesson in the 8th grade. We had observed colored fringes (refraction phenomena) while looking through any kind of prism at objects that had light surfaces that bounded dark surfaces. In class we developed the convention that one of the edges of the prism would always face upwards, and we all held our prisms at eye level so that we would all see the same order of colors when we all looked at the same boundary. Given this orientation of the prism, when the light surface was above the dark surface, the warm spectrum (red, orange, yellow) was observed, and when the dark surface was above the light surface, the cool spectrum (blue, violet) was observed. For homework that night, I gave each of the students a prism and asked them to draw a "scene" in their main lesson book of their own room at home.

The following day I asked the students to show me their drawings and received the following unexpected response from one of the students that sounded something like this: "It didn't work. I don't know what happened but I started to do the assignment and everything was going well and then it stopped working! Maybe something is wrong with my prism. I started to draw my wall with the window and at first there were the colors, just like yesterday. Then after awhile the colors started to get fainter and sort of disappeared, so I gave up. Then when I came back later to try and do it again the colors were back, only this time, the warm and cool colors were now switched from where they were before!"

I stood in the front of the class and pondered this statement for a few moments. I imagined her house, the time of year (December), and sensing what might have happened, proceeded with questions. "What time of day did you begin?"

"Late afternoon," she replied.

"Specifically what time?"

"I started about four in the afternoon and worked for half an hour."

"Is that when the problem started?"

"Yes, so I stopped and then tried again after dinner. That's when the colors switched."

I then turned to the class and asked them what had changed during that time. Eventually, the students realized that the sun was setting at that time and that their classmate had been working in a room without a light on. Under these conditions, the light colored window (there was snow on the ground, and her house was in an open field) and the relative darker coloration of the walls (in a room lit only from the sun outside) gave her one orientation of colors. As the sun set, everything in the room and the window began to appear dark so there were no longer any light/dark boundaries visible. When she returned from dinner it had become very dark. The class eventually realized their classmate had turned on her bedroom light so that now, the window was dark and the walls were light. These were the opposite conditions that she had started with and the reason for all of the difficulties that night!

What had happened in the class was remarkable. The frustrated student had given her classmates a real opportunity to understand the conditions for color fringe phenomena because she had observed something that at first appearance made no sense. In time, the class sorted out the mystery and the teacher's task was to simply find the right questions that would help the students discover the relationship out of their own efforts. Finally, the student who made the observation felt empowered by her discovery.

Using a conventional approach to science education, one usually begins with "the law" and then performs experiments or demonstrations to show its justification. In a class with a conventional approach to science, it would have been very easy to dismiss the experience above as something that did not fit "the law of refraction." This can send a student the message that the senses cannot be trusted. Yet, it was because people used their senses, and carefully so, that the lawfulness was found in the first place!

A Brief Comment on Bookwork

Finally, it is important for all students to make the experience and the discovered relationships their own. In the middle school years, a lot of time can be spent developing clear and orderly descriptions of what took place and what were the relationships that were uncovered. While these descriptions can be completed initially as a class together, in time each individual child should begin to develop a responsibility for his or her own record of "what happened."

In any case, the teacher should check and make suggestions on "first drafts" to ensure that each student is developing a clear relationship to observations, sequencing, and finding appropriate relationships. For some experiences, a detailed illustration might capture all of the phenomena and relationships and a written essay would be redundant.

In time, each teacher can develop a sense for the balance between written work and illustrations, rather than simply insisting that each demonstration must include both. By the end of the block, ideally each student will have a main lesson book that helps him or her to "remember" all of the experiences that were encountered and have a feeling (sense) for all of the relationships that were found.

Where Does This Lead? A Brief Sketch of Some Elements of the High School Physics Curriculum

Phenomena-based methods can continue to be used in high school and, from my experience, very successfully. If the students have a solid foundation in observation and stay attentive to the phenomena under consideration, then they can really delve into almost any topic in science and understand it in context.

For example, in 9th grade the students begin a study of thermal phenomena by performing a few experiments and then making clear distinctions between the concepts of heat and temperature. A modest beginning, no doubt. However, by the end of the second week of the block, the class will have progressed toward the solution of basic algebraic problems in thermal physics. For example, the students can calculate how warm a known mass of cool water in a bucket will get if a specific piece of hot copper is cooled by plunging it into the bucket. In our school the students perform this activity in the context of making a hammered copper bowl.

The physics block ends with a fairly thorough understanding of a four-stroke internal combustion engine. And yes, the students do disassemble an automobile engine before we speak about how it works.

In the 10th grade, the students develop the laws of mechanics and take up some of the same questions that Galileo wrestled with as pointed out earlier.

In the 11th grade, the students deal with the non-material world in physics, the field theories of electricity and magnetism. The students wrestle with forming concepts from experiments that can only tell us indirectly about what is being experienced. The electric or magnetic fields themselves are not visible. Yet we can see effects on sensible phenomena (objects) that tell us how these forces behave.

In our school the students also study atomic theory in the 11th grade. Now the students have the mental ability to really work with the phenomena as well as the conceptual framework that evolved into the atomic model of matter. What is more, by waiting so long to expose the students to this model, it is possible to take the students beyond the simplified version of this theory usually studied in more conventional science programs.

This means that in conjunction with the work on field theory described above, the students can now develop an appreciation for the general descriptions and ideas that are being discussed in even the most recent research, in which the experiments result in phenomena that have lost most of the qualities we normally associate with matter! Again, this can occur only when the students have developed a clear understanding of the distinction between the perceptual world of the senses and the conceptual world of the mind.

In the 12th grade, the students delve into visual phenomena. Now they can finally take on some of the philosophical questions that arise when we ask, "How do we see the world?" Or expressed in another form, "What is the foundation for knowing?"

Instrumentation and Equipment

As a final note, when speaking with parents about phenomen-ological methods, the question of instrumentation can often arise. Yes, electron microscopes and electric meters can be very useful tools for scientists and engineers. However, it is very easy for students, most adults and even many scientists to lose track of what is actually being observed. For example, the "image" created by an electron microscope appears to be an "object" but is in fact a visual representation of varying strengths of an electric field. While the distinction made can seem small, the implications of such statements can be tremendously important as one proceeds deeper into the sciences. Therefore, in the schools we want to use only equipment that students are able to understand with their present mode of consciousness. This implies simple equipment in the middle school years and somewhat more sophisticated instrumentation later on. Remember, the thinking capacities of the students have less to do with what instrumentation they can use and more to do with how they work with the observations they have made.

MICHAEL D'ALEO teaches Physics and Physical Sciences at the Waldorf School of Saratoga Springs in Saratoga Springs, NY, and is an instructor in the summer high school teacher training program at The Center for Anthroposophy in Wilton, NH. After being a class teacher for grades 6–8, he co-authored a book with Stephen Edelglass, Sensible Physics Teaching, a Guide for Teaching Physics in Grades 6–8. *Prior to teaching, Michael worked as a design and development engineer in the electronics industry and is listed as an inventor on seventeen U.S. Patents. He is currently the director of research for SENSRI, a non-profit scientific research group that investigates the methods and applications of phenomena-based science. Michael shepherds the Teaching Sensible Science workshop for the Research Institute of Waldorf Education, a course training practicing teachers in phenomenological science.*

The Results of Waldorf Education

What really are the results of Waldorf (Rudolf Steiner) education? You can be initially impressed by the enthusiasm and commitment of teachers in a Waldorf school and admire the artistic, environmental, scientific, and academic striving of the students. If you have the opportunity to visit a Waldorf school, you may observe joy in learning, attention devoted to emotional intelligence, and dynamic social interaction. The aesthetics of the classrooms, the students' artistic work, and the deliberate kinesthetic activities may capture your attention. But what happens to these students after they leave the idyllic environment of the Waldorf school? How do they find themselves prepared for life? What do they study in college? What do they do if they decide not to continue their formal education right away? How are they perceived by their employers, their professors ... and, maybe most importantly, how do they see themselves? These questions have been addressed in two studies published by the Research Institute for Waldorf Education. This pamphlet highlights some of these findings. However, you are strongly encouraged to read the original research in its entirety.*

For Phase II of its study, the Research Institute for Waldorf Education conducted online interviews with 526 former Waldorf students who graduated from 27 Waldorf high schools between 1943 and 2005. The surveys focused on where their paths after graduation led them, what form their educational paths had taken, and where they attended school after leaving high school. They were asked about

---

* See *Research on Waldorf Graduates in North America, Phase I*, Faith Baldwin, David Mitchell, Douglas Gerwin, New York, AWSNA Publications, 2005; and *Survey of Waldorf Graduates, Phase II*, David Mitchell, Douglas Gerwin, New York, AWSNA Publications, 2007.

their subsequent education, employment, values and life goals, as well as the quality of their personal relationships and health. College professors were also interviewed. Over half of the students referred to as "Waldorf graduates" experienced twelve years in a Waldorf school (more if they attended a Waldorf kindergarten). The following article presents a professor's personal view of Waldorf graduates.

The Waldorf Graduate:
A Personal Reflection

Dr. W. Warren B. Eickelberg
Professor of Biology
Director, Premedical Curriculum
Adelphi University
Garden City, New York

When I began teaching at Antioch University in the 1950s, no biologist even knew what a gene was, and now we manufacture them. When I entered teaching, there were but a dozen antibiotics, and now they number in the thousands. Back then many of the biological subdisciplines did not exist, and much of what we taught then would now be incorrect. The minds of men and women have opened for us new vistas to view; the hands of men and women have given us new technology, but the souls of men and women remain largely the same, always searching for the answers as to who we are, why we are here, and what our destiny is.

As there have been changes in academic content and technology, so the typical undergraduate student has changed. I lived with and experienced the job-oriented World War II veteran. I remember well the recall to active duty of many for the "peace action" in Korea. I sat through the "teach-ins" and the campus strikes of the Vietnam era. I lived through the revealing anatomy of the miniskirt, the drabness of the dark blue jeans phase, the demands by the students to develop their own curricula, the reorientation of learning by professors and administrators, the establishment of obviously immoral sex morés, the decline in admissions standards, and the unique and possibly devastating effect that the medium of television has had on young

I feel certain that all Waldorf school graduates believe in the orderliness of our universe, and they believe the human mind can discern this order and appreciate its beauty.

people. Without any doubt, my teaching experience has been marked by change, change, and ever more change.

Throughout this dynamism of activity where values were under attack and standards of behavior were challenged, from time to time there would be a unique stabilizing influence in my classes: a Waldorf school graduate. And they were different from the others. Without exception they were, at the same time, caring people, creative students, individuals of identifiable values, and students who, when they spoke, made a difference.

Let me share with the reader some of these features so that you too might see the difference. Almost without exception, every Waldorf school graduate has shown concern for the embalmed animals we use for dissection in Comparative Anatomy. I was always asked if the animal died painlessly, and they further questioned as to how. The Waldorf school graduates of the fifties, and of today, still show a unique reverence for life, and they regard an experimental animal, whether dead or alive, in a special way … not just another reagent or piece of equipment to use in a laboratory experiment. Whereas most students are surprised to see the giant liver of a shark, it is always the Waldorf school graduate who sees this massive organ filled with oils as the result of a unique plan to give an animal buoyancy.

When describing geologic time, I have often told the true story of a man whose calculator could record the number 9.9×10^{99}. He discovered that even the estimated number of atoms in the volume of our known universe in cubic millimeters could not begin to approach this order of magnitude. It was a Waldorf student who found an article suggesting that the chances of two human beings, other than identical twins, being genetically alike would approach one out of 1×10^{6270}, and thus concluded that indeed each person is a unique and specially created individual. We know the atoms in every cell of every living being are found in the stars and intergalactic gases and that we all make up a Community of Matter. As we in science view the universe from its creation to its predicted end, the human being may seem, astronomically speaking, rather insignificant, but any Waldorf school graduate will remind each of us that the human being is still the only astronomer. Once, when I was discussing the decreasing gene frequencies of Blood type B from Siberia through Western Europe, it was a Waldorf student who related this fact to the invasions by Genghis Khan and Tamerlane.

It has been said that historians see civilization as a stream through history, and the stream is often filled with blood, loud shouts, killing, and discoveries. Somehow it is the Waldorf school graduate who sees the stream, but also focuses on the banks where there are people who love, raise children, build homes, write poetry, carve statues, and worship. Waldorf school graduates see behind the facts that often must be repeated or explained on examination.

They are keenly interested in the macrocosm of the universe and microcosm of the cell's ultrastructure, but they know that Chemistry, Biology, and Physics cannot tell them much about the nature of love. In Embryology, they see a fetus develop a compound called prostaglandin to enhance the mother's response to oxytocin so that labor can begin, and they see this as a reflection of a guided universe. I feel certain that all Waldorf school graduates believe in the orderliness of our universe, and they believe the human mind can discern this order and appreciate its beauty.

Which Colleges Do Waldorf Graduates Attend?

Waldorf graduates have attended a wide range of colleges and universities around the world. In fact, it is notable that within a graduating class at a given school, generally very few people attend the same college as their classmates. In 2004 alone, the 438 Waldorf graduates who participated in the study attended 201 different colleges.

Which Types of Colleges Accept Waldorf Graduates?

A strikingly diverse number of institutions accept Waldorf graduates: in 2004, the 438 graduates were accepted at 342 different colleges. The Phase I study found that Waldorf graduates were accepted by 717 accredited colleges and universities, spanning 18 of the 20 types of institutions in the Carnegie Classification system.

An impressive majority of Waldorf school graduates pursue and complete degrees in higher education. 94% of the graduates taking part in this survey reported having attended college and 88% reported having completed or being in the process of completing a college or university level degree at the time of the survey. Of the remaining 12%, roughly half (5.4%) began but did not complete college, while the other half (6.3%) either did not pursue college or went into professional or artistic training unconnected with an academic degree program.

Where Do Waldorf Graduates Earn Their College Degrees?

*U.S. Colleges and Universities from which Waldorf Alumni/ae
Have Most Frequently Graduated*

1. Oberlin College
2. Hampshire College
3. University of California, Santa Cruz
4. Prescott College
5. Bennington College
6. University of California, Berkeley
7. Earlham College
8. Emerson College, Boston
9. Radcliffe College (and Harvard University)
10. Smith College
11. St. John's College
12. Temple University
13. Vassar College
14. Wesleyan University
15. Adelphi University
16. Amherst College
17. Boston University
18. Bowdoin College
19. Brown University
20. Cornell University

*Canadian Colleges and Universities from which Waldorf Alumni/ae
Have Most Frequently Graduated*

1. University of Toronto
2. University of British Columbia
3. Capilano College
4. Ontario College of Art and Design
5. Simon Fraser University
6. University of Victoria
7. Burlington College
8. California College of the Arts
9. Concordia University
10. Dalhousie University
11. Emily Carr Institute of Art and Design
12. McGill University
13. Memorial University of Newfoundland
14. Nova Scotia College of Art and Design
15. Seneca College
16. Toronto School of Homeopathic Medicine
17. Trent University
18. Vrije Universiteit, Amsterdam

A Sampling of Quotes from College Professors about Waldorf Graduates

Professors were asked to describe the Waldorf student(s) they had taught by comparison to other students in their classes. The following represent a few of the comments:

- Breadth of interest, willingness to explore new areas and to make connections to what was already known, artistic sense, and ability to apply it to scientific problems. Brought a strong, highly individualistic (non-sectarian) spiritual sense to her work—her world was larger and more interesting than herself.
  – Stan Rachootin, Professor of Biological Sciences
  Mt. Holyoke College

- Strong intellectual curiosity, a willingness to dive into and try out new things, an ability to empathize with students who are struggling, and the confidence to express herself.
  – Margaret Pobywajlo, PhD
  Director of the Learning Center
  University of New Hampshire, Manchester

- She understood that what the "crowd" was doing was a meaningless venture and she rejected it categorically. She did so without being snooty, loud, or stand-offish. But she did design a meaningful, basic foundation for her college education, which sets her miles apart from most students ANYWHERE.
  – Paula K. Clarke, PhD, Professor
  Columbia College

- Creative, responsible, inventive, resourceful, terrific storyteller with images and dialogue.
  – Iris Cahn, teacher, co-chair of
  Purchase College/SUNY Film Program

- She never seemed like a conventional student, and she was more than conventionally intelligent. While I recall, vividly, that her first few weeks at college were a trifle overwhelming, she came equipped with all the basic skills, and then some. She would never complete an assignment in a perfunctory way; she always did something to make her work special. But that was not to mask the quality of the work itself, which was very good—sometimes outstanding.

> – Carol Symes, Assistant Professor, Department of History
> University of Illinois at Urbana-Champaign

• Probably the unique thing [is the] remarkable seriousness and dedication to the academic life, its demands and its delights; it is very rare to see in such a young student.

> – Joseph Lauinger, Professor of Dramatic Literature
> Chairman, Literature Division, Sarah Lawrence College

• Blend of intelligence, compassion, organization and calmness under stress.

> – Nelson E. Bingham, PhD, Professor, Earlham College

• The intensity of her engagement in intellectual endeavors; her willingness to seek out unusual educational opportunities; the clarity of her thinking as she pulled together a diverse set of courses and experiences to shape her independent major.

> – Leslie Offutt, Vassar College

• His imagination, his nuanced verbal skills, and his leadership qualities.

> – Professor Bruce Bromley
> NYU lecturer in Expository Writing

• The tone of the discussions of [the Waldorf students I taught] always seemed to originate in a deeper source of awareness [of themselves] as feeling [human beings] than did those of their peers.

> – Jack Troy, Ceramics Professor, Juniata College

Fully 94% of the professors said *initiative* and *ethical standards* were among the strongest life skills demonstrated by Waldorf graduates. Similarly, 80% of the professors described the graduates as having *strong leadership skills*.

Waldorf graduates are perceived as thinking flexibly, often "outside the box" and able to integrate seemingly unrelated subjects with clarity and courage. Several professors commended the capacity to think flexibly with creative skills and specifically commented on Waldorf graduates' willingness to take intellectual risks.

In a time of rising plagiarism on college campuses (fueled by all manner of Internet services and ghost writers), it was striking to hear a professor say of a Waldorf undergraduate that "her social awareness is incredibly high, leadership excellent, ethical and moral standards stellar. I interact with many students. Her demeanor, skills, and social standards are the best I have encountered." Another professor described the Waldorf student she had taught as "a Renaissance man who has been able to find a balance between his intellectual gifts, his athletic interests, and his high ethical and moral standards."

Statistical Grading from 1–5 of Waldorf Graduates by College Professors with 5 Representing Outstanding

Quality	Average Ranking
Initiative	4.8
Social Awareness / Caring for Others	4.8
Communication	4.7
Speaking the Truth	4.7
Ethical Standards	4.6
Problem Solving	4.6
Judgment	4.4
Leadership Style and Effectiveness	4.4

Criticisms of Waldorf Graduates

Of the professors who supplied anecdotal observations, a majority said they had no concerns or criticism at all to offer when asked to identify the weaknesses in the Waldorf students they had taught compared with other students. A few noted some individual weaknesses in writing or computation, and a couple spoke of some emotional naïveté or youthfulness in their Waldorf students. Summing up some mild concerns about several Waldorf students he had taught over the years, one professor concluded, "Given a choice, I would love to educate a Waldorf student anytime."

One former Waldorf student criticized the education "for opening too many areas of interest." As a 28-year-old she and some of her friends found it hard to focus on one occupation because so much in life interested them.

Waldorf graduates strongly link the development of their social awareness to life in the Waldorf classroom, especially if they had been shepherded through the eight years of the elementary school by the same teacher. Though a few felt "stifled" by the small size of their classes, many reported how closely they related to their classmates and teachers, even to the point of staying in touch with them long after graduating from high school. The closeness of the students, in the words of one student, "forced all of us to overcome our differences and our grudges as quickly as we came by them and taught us how to work through trivial drama and value each other for our true potential."

There were a few graduates who were critical of the way they were taught science or of the emphasis placed on the arts, and there were others who felt insufficiently challenged due to the wide range of abilities among their classmates. But most graduates felt the full range of subjects required of all students served them well. In the words of one graduate, "It is the well-rounded approach that stands out the most. For me, exposure to the arts and music and learning by doing are the characteristic traits of Waldorf education." In the words of another graduate, "Waldorf education prepared me for anything and everything!"

Year Off Before College

In Phase I of the graduate survey, it was noted that 22.8% of Waldorf seniors who eventually attended college or university opted to take a year first to broaden their life experiences. This number is high because two thirds of the respondents from Canada took a thirteenth year program.

Some of the activities selected for this break in their education included:

* Became a stonemason building St. John's Cathedral in New York City
* Studied Buddhism at a Zen retreat for a year
* Worked at an orphanage in Africa
* Became a professional forester
* Traveled to Chile to study crafts
* Studied ballet in London, England
* Volunteered at ITESCO in Gaudalajara, Mexico
* Took a year in Italy to become fluent in Italian
* Traveled to Japan sponsored by Rotary International
* Attended culinary school
* Apprenticed with a fashion designer
* Traveled for two years with the "Up with People" program
* Acted in a lead role in a television series in New Zealand
* Apprenticed to a world famous painter in Vienna, Austria
* Fished commercially for crabs in Alaska
* Worked for a year to earn money for college
* Joined the Big Apple Circus
* Traveled throughout the United States by motorcycle
* Traveled and backpacked through Europe

Note: See *Research on Waldorf Graduates in North America, Phase I,* pp. 41–42, for a full list of activities.

Impressions of Waldorf Students from Their Employers

Waldorf graduates who entered the work force without starting or completing college were invited to give the names and contact details of their employers, who were then asked to offer anecdotal and statistical descriptions of the Waldorf graduates in their employ. These responses recognize Waldorf graduates for their "amazing creative side, their dependability, their leadership and social awareness," and their standing as a "model of ethical and moral standards."

Quotes from Employers about Waldorf Graduates Who Did Not Attend College

* Willingness to go "the extra mile," compatibility, compassion, and enthusiasm.
* If she says she is going to do something, she does it, [and does it] on time. She is willing to substitute for others if they cannot perform their tasks.
* Very flexible. Quick learner. Always picked up everything quickly.
* Continually trying to develop a deeper understanding and is open to new ideas, different aspects, and wider perspectives.
* Works with non-verbal and autistic children for whom she must intuit wishes and needs from non-verbal and other cues. She is thoughtful and caring towards her co-workers.

What Graduates Say about Their Waldorf Education

Self-development, wakefulness to social and community life, as well as balance or "wholeness" were the graduates' foremost memories of their Waldorf education.

I was asked to describe how my Waldorf education has served me in life—but that's like asking me how my heart has served me in life! It has been so essential. Now, I am not saying that knitting got me into Yale. But [Waldorf education] helped me develop a vitally important capacity which I would call "cognitive love"—the ability to embrace the world with one's thinking, to engage one's mind actively in loving dedication to a brighter future.

– Former Waldorf student from the Hartsbrook School

In high school I gained a foundation in real knowledge that is already evident in college. This is true in math and science, not just in art and history. In chemistry at Rochester Institute of Technology, I can explain to my classmates what happens when a particular acid and a particular base mix because we mixed those chemicals in 10th grade. Other students learned about acids and bases from textbooks, or their lab experience was not meaningful, and so they cannot picture what happens. Classmates and dorm friends constantly ask me how I know what I know—it's not that I know more facts than they do, but that I have remembered what I learned and I know how to connect facts to relate them to what I am doing.

– Former Waldorf student from the Great Barrington
Rudolf Steiner School

Occupations Pursued
(For those who did not attend or complete college)

Business	21.3%
Performing Arts	19.1%
Other (including military)	14.9%
Fine & Studio Arts	10.6%
Trades & Construction Management	8.5%
Education	8.5%
Health Care	6.4%
Administration	4.3%
Horticulture	4.3%
Technical Fields	2.1%

Occupations Underwritten
after Earning Undergraduate Degree

Ranked most to least frequent for all participants (1943–2005)

Education	14.1%
Fine and Studio Arts (including Architecture)	9.8%
Administration, Management, and Development	8.8%
Performing Arts (Broadcasting, Dance, Film, Music, Theater)	8.4%
Health and Medicine	8.0%
Business	6.9%
Various Professions and Trades	6.9%
Publishing, Journalism, and Writing	5.8%
Sciences and Technology	5.8%
Environment, Horticulture, and Agriculture	3.4%
Government, Politics, Lobbying, Planning	3.2%
Not-for-Profit and Volunteer	2.9%
Social and Human Services	2.7%
Advertising and Marketing	2.4%
Trades: Construction and Mechanical	2.4%
Engineering	1.9%
Retail	1.9%
Office and Clerical	1.6%
Law	1.3%
Raising Family	1.3%
Professional Athletics/Sports	0.5%

Comparison of Waldorf Students
to United States Student Population

Compared to the general U.S. population:
- Almost 3 times as many Waldorf graduates study social and behavioral sciences.
- About 50% more Waldorf graduates study science and math.
- Almost 3 times as many Waldorf graduates major in arts and humanities.

Profile of a Waldorf Graduate

- After graduating from Waldorf, attends college (94%)
- Majors in arts/humanities (47%) or sciences/math (42%) as an undergrad
- Graduates or is about to graduate from college (88%)
- Highly values interpersonal friendships (96%)
- Is self-reliant and highly values self confidence (94%)
- Highly values verbal expression (93%) and critical thinking (92%)
- Practices and values "lifelong learning" (91%)
- Highly values tolerance of other viewpoints (90%)
- Is highly satisfied in choice of occupation (89%)
- At work cares most about ethical principles (82%) and values helping others (82%)
- Expresses a high level of consciousness in making relationships work—both at home and at work

Three Key Findings about Waldorf Graduates

1. Waldorf graduates think for themselves and value the opportunity to translate their new ideas into practice. They both value and practice lifelong learning and have a highly developed sense for aesthetics.

2. Waldorf graduates value lasting human relationships, and they seek out opportunities to be of help to other people.

3. Waldorf graduates say they are guided by an inner moral compass that helps them navigate the trials and temptations of professional and private life. They carry high ethical principles into their chosen professions.

Made in the USA
Las Vegas, NV
25 November 2022